STUDY GUIDE

FOR

MANAGING HUMAN RESOURCES

16th Edition

Scott Snell

Professor of Business Administration,
University of Virginia

George Bohlander

Professor Emeritus of Management,
Arizona State University

Prepared by

John Bowen

Ohio State University, Newark
Columbus State Community College

SOUTH-WESTERN
CENGAGE Learning

Australia•Brazil•Japan•Korea•Mexico•Singapore•Spain•United Kingdom• United States

ISBN-13: 978-1-111-82492-1
ISBN-10: 1-111-82492-4

South-Western, Cengage Learning
5191 Natorp Boulevard
Mason, OH45040
USA

Cengage Learning is a leading provider of customized learning solutions with office locations around the globe, including Singapore, the United Kingdom, Australia, Mexico, Brazil, and Japan. Locate your local office at: **international.cengage.com/region**.

Cengage Learning products are represented in Canada by Nelson Education, Ltd.

For your course and learning solutions, visit **www.cengage.com**.

Purchase any of our products at your local college store or at our preferred online store **www.CengageBrain.com**.

Printed in the United States of America
1 2 3 4 5 6 7   15 14 13 12 11

TABLE OF CONTENTS

PREFACE

The student Study Guide that accompanies the 16th Edition of *Managing Human Resources* by Snell and Bohlander offers you the motivation to do well in this course. The objective of the student Study Guide is to increase your understanding of human resources management theory and concepts with a number of review features.

Learning Objectives. After you have read the chapter in the text, read the Learning Objectives to review what you should have learned from the chapter.

Chapter Summary. The Chapter Summary is prepared in conjunction with the learning objectives. Read and study the Chapter Summary carefully. Review any concepts in the text that you did not completely understand.

Self-Test Questions. The Self-Test section includes three separate self-test exercises—**Multiple Choice** questions, **True/False** questions, and a **Definition Review** in the form of matching questions. Test questions are both new and revised, and the Multiple Choice questions include real-life applications questions to improve your understanding of the business of human resource management as it relates to theoretical concepts. **Internet exercises** will add to your wealth of knowledge, and a **How To** section will help improve your understanding of the human resources function as it applies to recruitment, selection, orientation, and training, with a focus on continuous improvement through the creation of workforce diversity.

When reading and studying the textbook, use the opportunity to apply and integrate the knowledge you have gained to answer the questions that appear in this Study Guide.

Answers. The answers to all the Multiple Choice, True/False, and Definition Review Matching questions are found at the end of each chapter. Check your answers only after you have answered all of the questions. Reviewing any incorrect answers may suggest the need for further review of the text material. You can easily find the material in the textbook by using the learning objective icon that appears with each Multiple Choice and True/False question.

Have a great semester.

CHAPTER 1

THE CHALLENGE OF HUMAN RESOURCES MANAGEMENT

As a student you will learn how firms gain sustainable competitive advantage with and through people. You will be able to comprehend the concept of globalization and the impact it is having on human resources (HR) management. This awareness will provide a perspective with which to interpret current practices, problems, and issues more clearly. Chapter 1 is designed to make you aware of the challenges of human resources management that you will encounter in the work environment. In reading this chapter you will be able to understand how information technology challenges managers and employees. Also, you will become acquainted with the growing body of knowledge in the field. In this chapter, you will learn about the importance of change management, about the tools that are used by human resources managers (such as the development of intellectual capital), and about the ways total quality management (TQM) and reengineering challenge human resources systems. You will be able to learn the roles and competencies required by human resources managers. Finally, you will be able to understand the impact of cost pressures on human resources policies and the pertinence of changing demographics and employee concerns to human resources management.

LEARNING OUTCOMES

After studying this chapter, you should be able to

LEARNING OUTCOME 1	Explain how human resources managers can help their firms gain a sustainable competitive advantage through the strategic utilization of people.
LEARNING OUTCOME 2	Explain how globalization affects human resources management.
LEARNING OUTCOME 3	Explain how good human resources practices can help a firm achieve its corporate social responsibility and sustainability goals.
LEARNING OUTCOME 4	Describe how technology can improve how people perform and are managed.

LEARNING OUTCOME 5	Discuss how cost pressures affect human resources management policies.
LEARNING OUTCOME 6	Discuss how firms can leverage employee differences to their strategic advantage.
LEARNING OUTCOME 7	Explain how educational and cultural changes in the workforce are affecting human resources management.
LEARNING OUTCOME 8	Provide examples of the roles and competencies of today's HR managers.

CHAPTER SUMMARY RELATING TO LEARNING OUTCOMES

LEARNING OUTCOME 1 HR managers who have a good understanding of their firm's business can help it achieve its strategies—whatever they may be—through the effective utilization of people and their talents. An organization's success increasingly depends on the knowledge, skills, and abilities of its employees. To "compete through people," organizations have to do a good job of managing human capital: the knowledge, skills, and capabilities that have value to organizations. Managers must develop strategies for identifying, recruiting, and hiring the best talent available; developing these employees in ways that are firm-specific; helping them to generate new ideas and generalize them throughout the company; encouraging information sharing; and rewarding collaboration and teamwork among employees.

LEARNING OUTCOME 2 Globalization has become pervasive in the marketplace. It influences the number and kinds of jobs that are available and requires that organizations balance a complicated set of issues related to managing people working under different business conditions in different geographies, cultures, and legal environments. HR strategies and functions have to be adjusted to take into account these differences.

LEARNING OUTCOME 3 The fast pace of globalization along with corporate scandals over the years have led to a new focus on corporate social responsibility (good citizenship) and sustainability (a company's ability to produce a good or service without damaging the environment or depleting a resource). Companies are finding out that having a good reputation for pursuing these efforts can enhance their revenues and improve the caliber of talent they are able to attract. One of HR's leadership roles is to spearhead the development and implementation of corporate citizenship throughout their organizations, especially the fair treatment of workers.

LEARNING OUTCOME 4   Technology has tended to reduce the number of jobs that require little skill and to increase the number of jobs that require considerable skill, a shift we refer to as moving from touch labor to knowledge work. This displaces some employees and requires that others be retrained. In addition, information technology has influenced HRM through human resources information systems (HRIS) that streamline HR processes, make information more readily available to managers and employees, and enable HR departments to focus on the firm's strategies. The Internet and social media are also affecting how employees are hired, work, and are managed.

LEARNING OUTCOME 5   To contain costs, organizations have been downsizing, outsourcing, offshoring, furloughing, and leasing employees, as well as enhancing productivity. HR's role is to not only implement these programs but consider the pros and cons of programs such as these and how they might affect a company's ability to compete, especially if they lead to the loss of talented staff members.

LEARNING OUTCOME 6   The workforce is becoming increasingly diverse, and organizations are doing more to address employee concerns and to maximize the benefit of different kinds of employees. But to benefit from those differences managers need to look past the obvious differences between employees and see not so obvious differences such as how they think, learn, work, solve problems, manage their time, and deal with other people. By first seeing the differences, exploring them, and then discovering how they can provide value to the organization, HR managers can leverage those differences.

LEARNING OUTCOME 7   HR managers have to keep abreast of the educational abilities of the talent available to their organization. Despite the fact the educational attainment of the labor force has risen in general, many firms are finding it difficult to find workers with the basic skills they need. As the baby boomers retire, HR departments may have to offer higher compensation packages to attract qualified candidates, and recruiting and selection systems will have to function much more competitively. Employee rights, privacy concerns, attitudes toward work, and efforts to balance work and family are becoming more important to workers as the cultural dynamics in the labor force shift. Companies are finding that accommodating employees' individual needs as a result of these shifts is a powerful way to attract and retain top-caliber people.

LEARNING OUTCOME 8   In working with line managers to address their organization's challenges, HR managers play a number of important roles; they are called on for strategic advice and ethics counsel, various service activities, policy formulation and implementation, and employee advocacy. To perform these roles effectively, HR managers must have a deep understanding of their firm's operational, financial and personnel capabilities. HR managers who do and are creative and innovative can help shape a firm's strategies so as to respond successfully to changes in the marketplace. Ultimately, managing people is rarely the exclusive responsibility of the HR function. Every manager's job involves managing people. Consequently, successful companies combine the expertise of HR specialists with the experience of line managers and executives to develop and use the talents of employees to their greatest potential.

REVIEW QUESTIONS

Multiple Choice

Choose the letter of the word or phrase that best completes each statement.

Learning Outcome (LO)

LO 1 _____ 1. To "compete through people", organizations must do a good job of
a. managing the payroll.
b. managing human capital.
c. recognizing that people are competitive.
d. providing people with what they want.

LO 1 _____ 2. Human capital consists of
a. knowledge.
b. skills.
c. capabilities.
d. all of the above.

LO 1 _____ 3. A set of principles and practices whose core ideas include understanding customer needs, doing things right the first time, and striving for continuous improvement is
a. Total Quality Management (TQM).
b. Collective Bargaining.
c. Six Sigma.
d. Intellectual Capital.

LO 1 _____ 4. The fundamental rethinking and radical redesign of business processes to achieve dramatic improvements in cost, quality, service, and speed is referred to as
a. reengineering.
b. total quality management.
c. proactive management.
d. Six Sigma.

LO 1 _____ 5. The means organizations are using to modify the way they operate in order to be more successful are programs focused on
a. total quality.
b. continuous improvement.
c. reengineering.
d. all of the above.

LO 1 _____   6. When external forces have already affected an organization's
performance, the change is
   a. proactive.
   b. reactive.
   c. combative.
   d. disengaging.

LO 2 _____   7. Globalization requires that HR strategies consider
   a. how to avoid the impact of cultural differences.
   b. how to standardize business conditions.
   c. how to deal with different legal environments.
   d. how to avoid complicated issues.

LO 2 _____   8. In order to grow and prosper, many companies are seeking business
opportunities in
   a. global markets.
   b. industrial markets.
   c. domestic operations.
   d. employment markets.

LO 2 _____   9. Coca Cola generates most of its revenues
   a. overseas.
   b. in its home state of Georgia.
   c. from investments in securities.
   d. from the United States.

LO 2 _____   10. Approximately what percentage of the U.S. economy is affected
by international competition?
   a. 25-40.
   b. 40-55.
   c. 55-70.
   d. 70-85.

LO 2 _____   11. The first major trade agreement of the twentieth century, which
established rules and guidelines for global commerce between nations
and groups of nations, is called
   a. World Market Operations.
   b. Uniform Trade of Commerce.
   c. North American Free Trade Agreement.
   d. General Agreement on Tariffs and Trade (GATT).

LO 3 _____ 12. Concerns that people in developing economies and the world's environment are being exploited by companies in richer, more developed countries, coupled with numerous scandals plaguing U.S. corporations, have led to a new focus on
  a. environmental trade protection.
  b. uniform commerce and trade.
  c. corporate social responsibility.
  d. fair trade protection.

LO 4 _____ 13. The organizational challenge of the new millennium is
  a. e-commerce.
  b. tariffs and trade.
  c. industrial marketing.
  d. uniform trade practice.

LO 4 _____ 14. The introduction of advanced technology tends to increase the number of jobs that require
  a. less skill and knowledge.
  b. less know-how and work applications.
  c. greater responsibility with less pay.
  d. considerable skill.

LO 4 _____ 15. When employee responsibilities expand to include a richer array of activities such as planning, decision-making, and problem solving, the transformation has been referred to as
  a. collective bargaining.
  b. human resources information systems.
  c. job enrichment.
  d. "knowledge work."

LO 4 _____ 16. The most central use of technology in HRM is an organization's
  a. human resources information system (HRIS).
  b. collective bargaining process.
  c. Six Sigma program.
  d. HR outsourcing program.

LO 4 _____ 17. HRIS can be a potent weapon for
  a. lowering administrative costs.
  b. increasing productivity.
  c. speeding up response times.
  d. all of the above.

LO 4 _____   18. When an effective HRIS is implemented, perhaps the biggest advantage gained is that HR personnel are able to concentrate more effectively on the firm's
a. strategic direction.
b. collective bargaining process.
c. job enlargement program.
d. job enrichment program.

LO 5 _____   19. The planned elimination of jobs is termed
a. downsizing.
b. economic growth.
c. Six Sigma.
d. proactive management.

LO 5 _____   20. Hiring someone outside the company to perform tasks that could be done internally is referred to as
a. outsourcing.
b. employment leasing.
c. offshoring.
d. Six Sigma.

LO 5 _____   21. The controversial practice of moving jobs overseas is referred to as
a. subcontracting.
b. offshoring.
c. employee leasing.
d. outsourcing.

LO 6 _____   22. Being acutely aware of characteristics *common* to employees while also managing these employees as *individuals* is referred to as
a. Six Sigma.
b. outsourcing.
c. collective bargaining.
d. managing diversity.

LO 6 _____   23. By 2050, all of the following are expected to increase as a percent of the U.S. population except
a. Whites.
b. Hispanic/Latino.
c. African American.
d. Asian American.

7

LO 6 _____ 24. By 2018, those who are 65 and older will grow _____ faster the total labor force.
    a. two times.
    b. four times.
    c. seven times.
    d. ten times.

LO 7 _____ 25. Which of the following is not characteristic of today's employees?
    a. The top priority is moving up the corporate ladder.
    b. Eighty-six percent seek a balance of work-fulfillment and work-life balance.
    c. Their focus is on interesting work.
    d. They seek ways of living that are less complicated.

LO 7 _____ 26. A firm may be sued by the government if background checks for criminal backgrounds and credit history result in
    a. an increase in unemployment.
    b. a discriminatory effect on minority groups.
    c. embarrassment to job applicants.
    d. damage to a criminal investigation.

LO 7 _____ 27. About _____ percent of U.S. have only the minimal reading and writing abilities needed for work and daily living.
    a. 85 - 90
    b. 65 - 70
    c. 45 - 50
    d. 25 – 30

LO 8 _____ 28. A major activity of an HR Manager is to listen to employee concerns and represent their needs to managers. This role is referred to as
    a. advise and counsel.
    b. service.
    c. policy formulation and implementation.
    d. employee advocacy.

LO 8 _____ 29. In regards to committees scrutinizing executive pay
    a. HR managers frequently provide them with advice.
    b. they are especially concerned about the pay of HR executives.
    c. the committees avoid seeking the advice of HR managers since such advice would likely be self-serving.
    d. their conclusions are suspect since the committees are always appointed by the same executives who are being scrutinized.

LO 8 _____ 30. HR managers serve
      a. management.
      b. staff.
      c. a dual role with both of the above.
      d. no one other than the CEO.

True/False

Identify the following statements as True or False.

Learning Outcome (LO)

LO 1 _____ 1. All managers are responsible for at least some of the activities that fall into the category of human resources.

LO 1 _____ 2. The term *human resources* implies that people have capabilities that drive organizational performance (along with other resources such as money, materials, and information).

LO 1 _____ 3. HR has an internal focus on employees unlike those who deal with the customer and thus have a focus on competitive advantage.

LO 2 _____ 4. Due to globalization, culture is no longer an issue confronting HR managers.

LO 2 _____ 5. HR personnel are responsible for implementing training programs and development opportunities to enhance managers' understanding of foreign cultures and practices.

LO 2 _____ 6. Nearly 97 of U.S. exporters are multi-billion dollar corporations.

LO 2 _____ 7. As a result of globalization the national identities of products are becoming clearer.

LO 3 _____ 8. HR practices can help a firm achieve its corporate social responsibility and sustainability goals.

LO 3 _____ 9. Corporate Social Responsibility can be thought of as practicing good citizenship.

LO 3 _____ 10. Nine out of ten of those born in 1980s and 1990s say they would switch brands based on their perception of a firm's commitment to social responsibility.

LO 4 _____ 11. Technology, transportation, communications, and utilities industries tend to spend the least on training.

LO 4 _____ 12. Information technology has changed the face of HRM in the United States and abroad.

LO 4 _____ 13. All sorts of routine HR activities have seen some sort of automation.

LO 4 _____ 14. Companies are now using software to recruit, screen, and pre-test applicants online before hiring them.

LO 4 _____ 15. HR managers tend to look down upon social media and thus avoid its use in recruiting.

LO 5 _____ 16. Organizations are taking many approaches to lowering labor-related costs, including employee leasing, in an attempt to achieve productivity enhancements.

LO 5 _____ 17. The focus on increased productivity has declined during the Great Recession.

LO 5 _____ 18. Downsizing is still being regarded as a short-term fix when times are tough.

LO 5 _____ 19. HR's biggest concern at present regarding benefits are rising health care costs and the new health care laws.

LO 6 _____ 20. Differences among employees are a barrier to leveraging employees to their strategic advantage.

LO 6 _____ 21. By 2050 current minorities will be a majority of the population.

LO 7 _____ 22. Employers have a right to monitor employee e-mails from work.

LO 7 _____ 23. Employees are working less hours than at anytime since 1973.

LO 8 _____ 24. Human resources managers are a resource to whom managers can turn for policy interpretation.

LO 8 _____ 25. HR professionals must establish personal credibility in the eyes of both those who are internal and external to the firm.

Matching

Match each term with the proper definition.

Terms

a. change management	k. line managers
b. collaborative software	l. managing diversity
c. corporate social responsibility	m. offshoring
d. downsizing	n. outsourcing
e. employee leasing	o. furloughing
f. globalization	p. proactive change
g. human capital	q. reactive change
h. human resources information system (HRIS)	r. reengineering
i. human resources management (HRM)	s. Six Sigma
j. knowledge workers	t. total quality management (TQM)

Definitions

_____ 1. employees whose responsibilities are expanded to include a richer array of activities such as planning, decision-making, and problem solving.

_____ 2. change that occurs after external forces have already affected performance.

_____ 3. represents the knowledge, skills, and capabilities of individuals that have economic value to an organization.

_____ 4. set of principles and practices whose core ideas include understanding customer needs, doing things right the first time, and striving for continuous improvement.

_____ 5. contracting outside the organization to have work done that formerly was done by internal employees.

_____ 6. being aware of characteristics common to employees, while managing employees as individuals.

_____ 7. trend toward opening up foreign markets to international trade and investment.

_____ 8. change initiated by managers to take advantage of targeted opportunities.

_____ 9. the planned elimination of jobs within the organization.

_____ 10. computerized system that provides current and accurate data for purposes of control and decision making.

_____ 11. process of dismissing employees who are then hired by a leasing company and contracting with that company to lease back the employees.

_____ 12. the fundamental rethinking and radical redesign of business processes to achieve dramatic improvements in cost, quality, service, and speed.

_____ 13. good citizenship.

_____ 14. the process of bringing together different kinds of people to achieve a common purpose.

_____ 15. moving jobs overseas.

_____ 16. a process used to translate customer needs into a set of optimal tasks that are performed in concert with one another.

_____ 17. a systematic way of bringing about and managing both organizational changes and changes on the individual level.

_____ 18. software that allows workers to interface and share information with one another electronically.

_____ 19. non-HR managers who are responsible for overseeing the work of other employees.

_____ 20. a situation in which an organization asks or requires employees to take time off for either no pay or reduced pay.

Internet Exercises

List the functions of Human Resources Management from the following website: http://www.managementhelp.org/hr_mgmnt/hr_mgmnt.htm.

How can U.S. firms do business in India?

http://www.buyusa.gov/india/en/motm.html

How to Develop a Working Knowledge

In developing a working knowledge, you should focus on a multiskilled approach to prepare yourself for the job market. It is important to have good communication skills, computer skills, and decision-making and problem-solving skills.

Your working knowledge should be integrated with the core competencies of the organization. The core competencies should be part of the orientation and training you receive when you join an organization. These competencies, along with an emphasis on a customer-driven approach, should provide a competitive edge for the firm.

Everyone in the firm should understand and adhere to the cultural values of the organization as well as its philosophy of management. Each organization has its own management style, and you should recognize this and adapt to it. You should position yourself on a career track for advancement in the organization and take advantage of growth opportunities when they are available.

SOLUTIONS

Multiple Choice:	True/False:	Matching:
1. b	1. True	1. j
2. d	2. True	2. q
3. a	3. False	3. g
4. a	4. False	4. t
5. d	5. True	5. n
6. b	6. False	6. l
7. c	7. False	7. f
8. a	8. True	8. p
9. a	9. True	9. d
10. d	10. True	10. h
11. d	11. False	11. e
12. c	12. True	12. r
13. a	13. True	13. c
14. d	14. True	14. i
15. d	15. False	15. m
16. a	16. True	16. s
17. d	17. False	17. a
18. a	18. False	18. b
19. a	19. True	19. k
20. a	20. False	20. o
21. b	21. True	
22. d	22. True	
23. a	23. False	
24. d	24. True	
25. a	25. True	
26. b		
27. c		
28. d		
29. a		
30. c		

False Statements Made True

3. HR has a focus on competitive advantage.

4. Due to globalization, culture is an issue confronting HR managers.

6. Nearly 97 percent of U.S. exporters are **smaller** firms.

7. As a result of globalization the national identities of products are becoming **less** clear.

11. Technology, transportation, communications, and utilities industries tend to spend the **most** on training.

15. HR managers tend to **use** social media in recruiting.

17. The focus on increased productivity has declined during the Great Recession.

18. Downsizing is **not just being used** as a short-term fix when times are tough.

20. Differences among employees are a **benefit in** leveraging employees to their strategic advantage.

23. Employees are working **more** hours than at anytime since 1973.

CHAPTER 2

STRATEGY AND HUMAN RESOURCES PLANNING

In this chapter you will understand how human resources planning and strategy efforts should be integrated. You will understand various stages of the strategic management process. You will comprehend the importance of internal resource analysis and have knowledge of basic tools of human resource forecasting. You will learn the importance of formulating and implementing the appropriate strategies. You will also recognize methods for assessing and measuring the effectiveness of a firm's strategy.

LEARNING OUTCOMES

After studying this chapter, you should be able to

LEARNING OUTCOME 1 Identify the advantages of integrating human resources planning and strategic planning.

LEARNING OUTCOME 2 Understand how an organization's competitive environment influences its strategic planning.

LEARNING OUTCOME 3 Understand why it is important for an organization to do an internal resource analysis.

LEARNING OUTCOME 4 Describe the basic tools used for human resources forecasting.

LEARNING OUTCOME 5 Explain the linkages between competitive strategies and HR.

LEARNING OUTCOME 6 Understand what is required for a firm to successfully implement a strategy.

LEARNING OUTCOME 7 Recognize the methods for assessing and measuring the effectiveness of a firm's strategy.

CHAPTER SUMMARY RELATING TO LEARNING OUTCOMES

LEARNING OUTCOME Strategic human resources management (SHRM) integrates strategic planning and HR planning. It can be thought of as the pattern of human resources deployments and activities that enable an organization to achieve its strategic goals. HR planning and strategies need to be continually monitored and assessed, especially when organizations consider global strategies, outsourcing, mergers, joint ventures, offshoring, the relocation of plants, product innovations, and downsizing, or when dramatic shifts in the composition of the labor force are occurring.

LEARNING OUTCOME 2 Analyzing the firm's competitive environment is central to strategic planning. The competitive environment includes the specific organizations with which the firm interacts. Firms analyze the competitive environment in order to adapt to or influence the nature of competition.

LEARNING OUTCOME 3 Conducting an internal analysis to gauge the firm's strengths and weaknesses involves looking at the firm's "three Cs"—its capabilities, composition and culture. An internal analysis enables strategic decision makers to assess the organization's workforce—its skills, cultural beliefs, and values. An organization's success increasingly depends on the knowledge, skills, and abilities of employees, particularly as they help establish a set of core capabilities that distinguish an organization from its competitors. When employees' talents are valuable, rare, difficult to imitate, and organized, a firm can achieve a sustained competitive advantage through its people.

LEARNING OUTCOME 4 HRP is a systematic process that involves forecasting demand for labor, performing supply analysis, and balancing supply and demand considerations. Forecasting demand requires using either quantitative or qualitative methods to identify the number and type of people needed to meet organizational objectives. Supply analysis involves determining whether sufficient employees are available within the organization to meet demand and whether potential employees are available on the job market.

LEARNING OUTCOME 5 As organizations plan for their future, top management and strategic planners must recognize that strategic-planning decisions affect—and are affected by—HR functions. Via HRP, human resources managers can proactively identify and initiate programs needed to develop organizational capabilities upon which future strategies can be built. HRP and strategic planning tend to be most effective when there is a reciprocal relationship between the two processes.

LEARNING OUTCOME 6 Formulating an HR strategy is only half of the HR battle. The strategy must also be implemented. Employment forecasts must be reconciled against the internal and external supplies of labor the firm faces. This can include having current employees work overtime, hiring full–time, part-time, or contract employees, downsizing employees; furloughing them; and outsourcing or offshoring. If there is a labor shortage, the firm might have to reformulate its long-and short-term strategic plans or find ways to develop employees "from the ground up."

LEARNING OUTCOME 7   Firms need to establish a set of parameters that focus on the "desired outcomes" of strategic planning, as well as the metrics they will use to monitor how well the firm delivers against those outcomes. Issues of measurement, benchmarking, alignment, fit, and flexibility are central to the evaluation process. Firms use benchmarking, strategy mapping, and the Balanced Scorecard (BSC) as tools to gauge outcomes.

REVIEW QUESTIONS

Multiple Choice

Choose the letter of the word or phrase that best completes each statement.

Learning Outcome (LO)

LO 1 _____   1. A set of procedures for making decisions about the organization's long-term goals and strategies involves
   a. strategic planning.
   b. human resources planning (HRP).
   c. succession planning.
   d. comprehensive planning.

LO 1 _____   2. The process of anticipating and making provisions for the movement of people into, within, and out of an organization is
   a. succession planning.
   b. human resources planning (HRP).
   c. strategic planning.
   d. comprehensive planning.

LO 1 _____   3. The combination of strategic planning and HR planning is
   a. value creation.
   b. strategic vision.
   c. strategic human resources management (SHRM).
   d. succession planning.

LO 1 _____   4. The first step in strategic planning is establishing
   a. a mission.
   b. a vision.
   c. values for the organization.
   d. all of the above.

17

LO 1 _____ 5. The strong enduring beliefs and principles that the company uses as a foundation for its decisions are its
    a. core values.
    b. strategies.
    c. operating facilities.
    d. innovations.

LO 2 _____ 6. The second component of the strategic management process is
    a. analysis of internal opportunities.
    b. analysis of external opportunities and threats.
    c. its external audits.
    d. the organization's external component.

LO 2 _____ 7. The systematic monitoring of the major external forces influencing the organization is
    a. environmental scanning.
    b. human resources planning.
    c. strategic planning.
    d. organizational analysis.

LO 3 _____ 8. Integrated skills and knowledge sets within an organization that distinguish it from its competitors and deliver value to customers are its
    a. operating plans.
    b. strategic plans.
    c. core capabilities.
    d. objectives.

LO 3 _____ 9. Which of the following programs are designed to motivate and spark creativity of workers?
    a. empowerment programs.
    b. total quality initiatives.
    c. continuous improvement efforts.
    d. all of the above.

LO 3 _____ 10. Companies tend to make long-term commitments to these employees, investing in their continuous training and development and perhaps giving them an equity stake in the organization.
    a. submarginal employees.
    b. operating employees.
    c. strategic knowledge Workers.
    d. management personnel.

LO 3 _____   11. This group of individuals has skills that are unique but frequently not directly related to a company's core strategy.
    a. Core Knowledge Workers.
    b. Alliance Partners.
    c. operating employees.
    d. management personnel.

LO 4 _____   12. What ultimately determines which forecasting technique will be used within an organization?
    a. organizational demands.
    b. staffing tables.
    c. replacement charts.
    d. skill inventories.

LO 4 _____   13. One example of a quantitative approach to forecasting that relies on a single factor is
    a. Markov analysis.
    b. staffing tables.
    c. replacement charts.
    d. trend analysis.

LO 4 _____   14. The opinions (judgments) of supervisors, department managers, experts, or others knowledgeable about the organization's future employment needs are
    a. management forecasts.
    b. core competencies.
    c. strategic visions.
    d. value creations.

LO 4 _____   15. Graphic representations of all organizational jobs, along with the numbers of employees currently occupying those jobs (and perhaps future employment requirements derived from demand forecasts), are
    a. replacement charts.
    b. skill inventories.
    c. staffing tables.
    d. organization charts.

LO 4 _____   16. An analysis that shows the percentage (and actual number) of employees who remain in each job from one year to the next as well as the proportions of those who are promoted, demoted, transferred, or exit the organization is called
    a. trend analysis.
    b. Markov analysis.
    c. SWOT analysis.
    d. core analysis.

LO 4 _____ 17. A technique that lists each employee's education, past work experience, vocational interests, specific abilities and skills, compensation history, and job tenure is called
    a. replacement charts.
    b. Markov analysis.
    c. value creation.
    d. skill inventories.

LO 4 _____ 18. Both skill and management inventories—broadly referred to as talent inventories—can be used to develop employee
    a. core values.
    b. core competencies.
    c. organizational capability.
    d. replacement charts.

LO 4 _____ 19. The process of identifying, developing, and tracking key individuals so that they may eventually assume top-level positions is
    a. strategic planning.
    b. management planning.
    c. succession planning.
    d. human resources planning.

LO 5 _____ 20. A comparison of strengths, weaknesses, opportunities, and threats normally is referred to as a
    a. SWOT analysis.
    b. Markov analysis.
    c. trend analysis.
    d. economic forecast.

LO 5 _____ 21. Sometimes firms do not acquire or merge with another firm, but instead pursue cooperative strategies such as a
    a. partnership.
    b. takeover.
    c. strategic alliance.
    d. missionary statement.

LO 5 _____ 22. A strategy based on high product quality, innovative features, speed to market, or superior service is a
    a. realignment strategy.
    b. differentiation strategy.
    c. human resources plan.
    d. strategic plan.

LO 6 _____   23. When forecasts show a surplus of employees, organizations may
  a. restrict hiring.
  b. reduce work hours.
  c. consider layoffs.
  d. all of the above.

LO 6 _____   24. A gradual reduction of employees through resignations, retirements, and deaths is called
  a. attrition.
  b. outsourcing.
  c. layoffs.
  d. offshoring.

LO 7 _____   25. The process of identifying "best practices" in a given area—say, productivity, logistics, brand management, training, etc.—and then comparing your practices and performance to those of other companies is
  a. benchmarking.
  b. strategy mapping.
  c. strategic planning.
  d. skill inventories.

LO 7 _____   26. According to Mark Huselid, a competitive advantage is based on a unique combination of a company's human capital, strategy, and
  a. internal fit.
  b. skills inventory.
  c. core capabilities.
  d. organizational flexibility.

LO 7 _____   27. One of the most enthusiastically adopted tools for mapping a firm's strategy in order to ensure strategic alignment is the
  a. trend analysis.
  b. Markov analysis.
  c. Balanced Scorecard (BSC).
  d. SWOT analysis.

LO 7 _____   28. The four related cells of the Balanced Scorecard are financial, customer, process, and
  a. people.
  b. resources.
  c. learning
  d. capacity.

Managing Human Resources

LO 7 _____   29. What kind of flexibility occurs through rapid reallocation of resources to new or changing needs?
    a. coordination flexibility
    b. resource flexibility
    c. capability flexibility
    d. planning flexibility.

LO 7 _____   30. What kind of flexibility occurs as a result of having people who can do many different things in different ways?
    a. coordination flexibility
    b. resource flexibility
    c. capability flexibility
    d. planning flexibility.

True/False

Identify the following statements as True or False.

Learning Outcome (LO)

LO 1 _____   1. Dramatic shifts in the composition of the labor force require that managers become less involved in planning.

LO 1 _____   2. The vision is the basic purpose of the organization, as well as its scope of operations.

LO 1 _____   3. Although the terms *mission* and *vision* often are used interchangeably, the mission statement ideally clarifies the long-term direction of the company and its strategic intent.

LO 2 _____   4. While there are many factors in the general environment that may influence strategic decisions, analysis of the firm's competitive environment is central to strategic planning.

LO 2 _____   5. One of the most important assessments a firm can make is identifying the needs of its employees.

LO 2 _____   6. At times, the biggest opportunity or threat in an industry comes from direct competition.

LO 2 _____   7. According to the U.S. Census Bureau, employment growth will continue to be concentrated in the manufacturing sector.

LO 2 _____   8. According to the U.S. Census Bureau, between 2006-2016, youths (16-24 years old) will see their share of the labor force fall.

LO 3 _____ 9. Because managers increasingly understand that employee-oriented cultures are critical to success, they often conduct cultural audits to examine the attitudes and beliefs of the workforce as well as the activities they engage in.

LO 3 _____ 10. In many cases, products are a key resource that underlies a firm's core capabilities.

LO 3 _____ 11. People are a source of competitive advantage when employee capabilities and contributions can be copied by others.

LO 3 _____ 12. Skill groups in any given organization can be classified according to the degree to which they create strategic value and are unique to the organization.

LO 3 _____ 13. Contract laborers have skills that are quite valuable to a company, but not particularly unique.

LO 4 _____ 14. Ideally forecasting should use only qualitative methods.

LO 4 _____ 15. Forecasting is frequently more a science than an art.

LO 4 _____ 16. Qualitative approaches to forecasting are more statistical than quantitative approaches.

LO 4 _____ 17. A qualitative forecasting method, the Delphi technique, attempts to decrease the subjectivity of forecasts by soliciting and summarizing the judgments of a pre-selected group of individuals.

LO 4 _____ 18. Ideally, forecasting should include the use of both quantitative and qualitative approaches.

LO 5 _____ 19. SWOT analysis helps executives summarize the major facts and forecasts derived from the external and internal analyses.

LO 5 _____ 20. Some estimates suggest that only about 50 percent of all mergers achieve their objectives (measured by return on investment, shareholder value, and the like).

LO 5 _____ 21. Companies can increase customer value by either decreasing costs to customers or increasing their benefits (or some combination).

LO 6 _____ 22. In the case of unionized organizations, the criteria for determining an employee's eligibility for layoff are typically set forth in the union agreement.

LO 7 _____ 23. The target company for benchmarking needs to be a competitor.

LO 7 _____ 24. Resource flexibility occurs through rapid reallocation of resources to new or changing needs.

LO 7 _____ 25. Resource flexibility results from having people who can do many different things in different ways.

Matching

Match each term with the proper definition.

Terms

a.	Balanced Scorecard (BSC)	o.	skill inventories
b.	benchmarking	p.	staffing tables
c.	core capabilities	q.	strategic planning
d.	core values	r.	strategic vision
e.	cultural audits	s.	succession planning
f.	environmental scanning	t.	SWOT analysis
g.	human capital readiness	u.	trend analysis
h.	human resources planning (HRP)	v.	value creation
i.	management forecasts	w.	values-based hiring
j.	Markov analysis	x.	
k.	mission	y.	
l.	organizational capability		
m.	quality of fill		
n.	replacement charts		

Definitions

_____ 1. integrated knowledge sets within an organization that distinguish it from its competitors and deliver value to customers.

_____ 2. the basic purpose of the organization as well as its scope of operations.

_____ 3. the procedures for making decisions about the organization's long-term goals and strategies.

_____ 4. the process of comparing the organization's processes and practices with those of other companies.

_____ 5. the systematic monitoring of the major external forces influencing the organization.

_____ 6. the opinions (judgments) of supervisors, department managers, experts, or others knowledgeable about the organization's future employment needs.

_____ 7. graphic representations of all organizational jobs, along with the numbers of employees currently occupying those jobs (and future employment requirements).

_____ 8. process of identifying, developing, and tracking key individuals for executive positions.

_____ 9. files of personnel education, experience, interests, skills, etc., that allow managers to quickly match job openings with employee backgrounds.

_____ 10. process of anticipating and making provisions for the movement of people into, within, and out of an organization.

_____ 11. listings of current job holders and persons who are potential replacements if an opening occurs.

_____ 12. a comparison of strengths, weaknesses, opportunities, and threats for strategy formulation purposes.

_____ 13. a quantitative approach to forecasting labor demand based on an organization index such as sales.

_____ 14. method for tracking the pattern of employee movements through various jobs.

_____ 15. a metric designed to measure how well new hires that fill positions are performing on the job.

_____ 16. the strong enduring beliefs and principles that the company uses as a foundation for its decisions.

_____ 17. a statement about the direction the company is taking and what it can become in the future; clarifies the long-term direction of the company and its strategic intent.

_____ 18. audits of the culture and quality of work life in an organization.

_____ 19. capacity of the organization to act and change in pursuit of sustainable competitive advantage.

_____ 20. what the firm adds to a product or service by virtue of making it; the amount of benefits provided by the product or service once the costs of making it are subtracted.

_____ 21. A tool for mapping a firm's strategy in order to ensure strategic alignment.

_____ 22. what the firm can understand once both the supply and demand for employee skills, talent, and know-how.

_____ 23. the process of outlining the behaviors that exemplify a firm's corporate culture and then hiring people who are a fit for them.

Internet Exercises

Workforce planning is a systematic approach to anticipating staffing needs and determining what activity should be undertaken to meet these needs. What does this multistep process involve?
http://www.suite101.com/article.cfm/human_resources/89522

Why is benchmarking a continual process?
http://www.pwc.com/extweb/service.nsf/docid/D70EBAA20A19F91F80256C2200321497

How to Write a Résumé and Search for a Job

It is important to prepare and market yourself for a job before graduating from your educational institution. Most colleges and universities have a placement office, and you should contact this office before graduation. Services provided by this office include the following:

- **résumé writing**
- **portfolio development**
- **interview coaching**
- **tapping the hidden job market**
- **job searching using the Internet**

Before graduation you should inquire about cooperative education to gain field experience through an internship, an externship, a practicum, a clinical placement, and other job-related experiences. It is difficult for a student to market a degree without any field experience.

You should attend workshops, annual job fairs, and career counseling services before graduation.

Review and analyze a job requisition booklet before you enter the labor market. Remember that it is your responsibility to contact the placement counselors at your school, so that they may assist in your career development program.

SOLUTIONS

Multiple Choice:	True/False:	Matching:
1. a	1. False	1. c
2. b	2. False	2. k
3. c	3. False	3. q
4. d	4. True	4. b
5. a	5. False	5. f
6. b	6. False	6. i
7. a	7. False	7. p
8. c	8. True	8. s
9. d	9. True	9. o
10. c	10. False	10. h
11. b	11. False	11. n
12. a	12. True	12. t
13. d	13. False	13. u
14. a	14. False	14. j
15. c	15. False	15. m
16. b	16. False	16. d
17. d	17. True	17. r
18. d	18. True	18. e
19. c	19. True	19. l
20. a	20. False	20. v
21. c	21. True	21. a
22. b	22. True	22. g
23. d	23. False	23. w
24. a	24. False	
25. a	25. True	
26. c		
27. c		
28. c		
29. a		
30. b		

False Statements Made True

1. Dramatic shifts in the composition of the labor force require managers to become **more** involved in planning.

2. The **mission** is the basic purpose of the organization, as well as its scope of operations.

3. Although the terms *mission* and *vision* are often used interchangeably, the **vision** statement ideally clarifies the long-term direction of the company and its strategic intent.

5. One of the most important assessments a firm can make is identifying the needs of its **customers**.

6. At times, the biggest opportunity or threat in an industry **does not** come from direct competition, **but from substitution**.

7. According to the U.S. Census Bureau, employment growth will continue to be concentrated in the **service-providing** sector.

10. In many cases, **people** are a key resource that underlies a firm's core capabilities.

11. People are a source of competitive advantage when employee capabilities and contributions **cannot** be copied by others.

13. **Core employees** have skills that are quite valuable to a company, but not particularly unique.

14. Ideally forecasting should include **both quantitative and qualitative** methods.

15. Forecasting is frequently more an **art** than a **science**.

16. Qualitative approaches to forecasting are **less** statistical than quantitative approaches.

20. Some estimates suggest that only about **15 percent** of all mergers achieve their objectives (measured by return on investment, shareholder value, and the like).

23. The target company for benchmarking **does not** need to be a competitor.

24. **Coordination** flexibility occurs through rapid reallocation of resources to new or changing needs.

CHAPTER 3

EQUAL EMPLOYMENT OPPORTUNITY AND HUMAN RESOURCES MANAGEMENT

In this chapter you will learn how managers must be constantly aware of the laws and regulations governing the employment relationship. This is true for both federal and state regulations. Many of these laws concern the fair and equal employment of protected classes of workers, although equal employment opportunity (EEO) laws pertain to all members of the labor force. You will understand from this chapter that equal employment opportunity laws cover all aspects of employment, including recruitment, selection, training, promotion, and compensation. In hiring or supervising employees, you will know to give careful attention to the application of equal employment opportunity laws and regulations to prevent charges of discrimination. Finally, you will be able to distinguish how protected classes can sustain a charge of adverse impact, how an employer can establish a defense of adverse impact, and how the employer should establish an affirmative action program.

LEARNING OUTCOMES

After studying this chapter, you should be able to

LEARNING OUTCOME 1	Explain the reasons behind passage of equal employment opportunity (EEO) legislation.
LEARNING OUTCOME 2	Prepare an outline describing the major EEO laws and the employment practices they prohibit. Describe what a bona fide occupational qualification is.
LEARNING OUTCOME 3	Understand why sexual harassment, immigration reform, and other practices such as discrimination based on a person's weight, appearance, and sexual orientation have become equal employment issues.

LEARNING OUTCOME 4   Explain how the *Uniform Guidelines on Employee Selection Procedures* were developed and how firms use them to ensure they are abiding by the law.

LEARNING OUTCOME 5   Understand the concepts of adverse impact and disparate treatment.

LEARNING OUTCOME 6   Understand EEOC record-keeping and posting requirements.

LEARNING OUTCOME 7   Describe how discrimination charges are processed by the EEOC.

LEARNING OUTCOME 8   Explain what affirmative action is and how companies today are seeing the value of voluntarily having diverse workforces.

CHAPTER SUMMARY RELATING TO LEARNING OUTCOMES

LEARNING OUTCOME   Employment discrimination against blacks, Hispanics, women, and other groups has long been practiced by U.S. employers. Prejudice against minority groups is a major cause in their lack of employment gains. Government reports show that the wages and job opportunities of minorities typically lag behind those for whites.

LEARNING OUTCOME 2   Effective management requires knowing the legal aspects of the employment relationship, including the laws and various executive orders mentioned in this chapter. Employers are permitted to discriminate against protected classes when doing so constitutes a reasonable business necessity or would impose an undue hardship, or when a bona fide occupational qualification for normal business operation exists.

LEARNING OUTCOME 3   Sexual harassment is an area of particular importance to managers and supervisors. Extensive efforts should be made to ensure that both male and female employees are free from all forms of sexually harassing conduct. The Immigration Reform and Control Act was passed to control unauthorized immigration into the United States. The law requires managers to maintain various employment records, and they must not discriminate against job applicants or employees because of their national origin or citizenship status. Other areas of discrimination that are or could become a concern for the EEOC in the future are discrimination based on people's weight, their appearance, or their status as a caregiver.

LEARNING OUTCOME 4   The *Uniform Guidelines on Employee Selection Procedures* is designed to help employers comply with federal bans against employment practices that discriminate on the basis of race, color, religion, gender, or national origin. The *Uniform Guidelines* provides employers with a framework for making legally enforceable employment decisions. Employers must be able to show that their selection procedures are valid when it comes to predicting a person's job performance.

LEARNING OUTCOME 5   Adverse impact plays an important role in proving employment discrimination. Adverse impact means that an employer's employment practices unintentionally resulted in the rejection of a significantly higher percentage of members of minority and other protected groups. By contrast, disparate treatment is intentional discrimination against a protected group. Refusing to hire individuals of a particular religion or denying males, but not females, clerical jobs are examples of disparate treatment discrimination.

LEARNING OUTCOME 6   To ensure that organizations comply with antidiscrimination legislation, the EEOC was established to monitor employers' actions. Employers subject to federal laws must maintain certain records and report certain employment statistics where mandated. Employers with 100 or more employees must file an EEO-1 report annually. This comprehensive document identifies employees by race/ethnicity and gender for ten job categories. Companies with government contracts of $50,000 or more must file an affirmative action plan with the OFCCP. Employers are required to collect employment data and file reports under various federal and state laws. Employers are also required to post in prominent locations EEO-related posters.

LEARNING OUTCOME 7   Employees or applicants for employment who believe they have been discriminated against may file a discrimination complaint (a charge form) with the EEOC. The employer receives a copy of the charge form that initiates an EEOC investigation of the alleged discrimination. Individuals claiming discrimination must file the complaint within 180 days of the alleged offense. After the investigation, if the Commission dismisses the charge, the plaintiff will receive a right-to-sue notice that allows the individual to start private litigation. If the EEOC finds reasonable cause for the charge, it will attempt to mediate a settlement between the parties. If an agreement is not reached, the EEOC may elect to sue the employer in federal court. Figure 3.6 illustrates the steps in filing a discrimination charge.

LEARNING OUTCOME   Affirmative action goes beyond providing equal employment opportunities to employees. Firms with federal contracts and firms that have been found guilty of past discrimination can be required to utilize affirmative action programs. This is accomplished by employing protected classes for jobs in which they are underrepresented. The employer's goal is to have a balanced internal workforce representative of the employer's relevant labor market. The future of affirmative action might not rest in judicial decisions or laws but in the efforts of managers to voluntary embrace and foster diversity. Differences of all sorts among people are ubiquitous in the workforce. Managers need to leverage these differences because they can be the source of organizational strength.

REVIEW QUESTIONS

Multiple Choice

Choose the letter of the word or phrase that best completes each statement.

Learning Outcome (LO)

LO 1 _____
1. The treatment of individuals in all aspects of employment, hiring, promotion, training, etc., in a fair and nonbiased manner is
   a. equal employment opportunity.
   b. sexual harassment.
   c. age discrimination.
   d. the four-fifths rule.

LO 1 _____
2. A central aim of political action has been to establish justice for all people of the nation through the protection of the
   a. United States Constitution.
   b. Fair Labor Standards.
   c. Equal Pay Act.
   d. Uniform Commercial Partnership Act.

LO 2 _____
3. Major federal EEO laws have attempted to correct social problems of interest to particular groups of workers called
   a. affirmative action.
   b. knowledge workers.
   c. protected classes.
   d. bona fide occupational qualification.

LO 2 _____
4. The act that outlaws discrimination in pay, employee benefits, and pensions based on the worker's gender is the
   a. Equal Employment Opportunity Act.
   b. Equal Pay Act.
   c. Age Discrimination in Employment Act.
   d. Americans with Disabilities Act.

LO 2 _____
5. The Equal Pay Act was passed as an amendment to the
   a. Equal Employment Opportunity Act.
   b. Equal Pay Act.
   c. Age Discrimination in Employment Act.
   d. Fair Labor Standards Act.

LO 2 _____   6. The Civil Rights Act of 1964 and the Civil Rights Act of 1991 cover a
broad range of organizations, *except*
a. all private employers in interstate commerce who employ fifteen or
more employees.
b. all foreign organizations doing business in their domestic countries.
c. state and local governments.
d. private and public employment agencies, including the U.S.
Employment Service.

LO 2 _____   7. Under Title VII of the Civil Rights Act, employers are permitted limited
exemptions from antidiscrimination employment preferences based on a
a. commercial code.
b. past practice.
c. common law.
d. bona fide occupational qualification.

LO 2 _____   8. A practice that is necessary for the safe and efficient operation of the
organization, as interpreted by the courts, is a defense based on
a. religious preference.
b. self-defense.
c. business necessity.
d. age discrimination.

LO 2 _____   9. The Pregnancy Discrimination Act affects employees' benefit programs
in the following areas, *except*
a. hospital and major medical insurance.
b. vacation and holiday pay.
c. temporary disability and salary continuation plans.
d. sick leave policies.

LO 2 _____   10. Discrimination against the disabled was first prohibited in federally
funded activities by the
a. The Pregnancy Discrimination Act.
b. Vocational Rehabilitation Act.
c. Americans with Disabilities Act.
d. Civil Rights Act.

LO 2 _____   11. In *Toyota v Williams,* the Supreme Court ruled that if a physical or
mental impairment is correctable, then it is not a
a. competitive reaction.
b. disability.
c. mental impairment.
d. physical disease.

33

LO 2 _____ 12. An attempt by employers to adjust, without undue hardship, the working conditions or schedules of employees with disabilities or religious preferences is based on
    a. reasonable accommodation.
    b. labor contracts.
    c. fairness and inequities.
    d. job analysis.

LO 3 _____ 13. Unwelcome advances, requests for sexual favors, and other verbal or physical conduct of a sexual nature constitutes
    a. fraud.
    b. antidiscrimination.
    c. sexual harassment.
    d. misrepresentation of fact.

LO 3 _____ 14. Illegal _____ has/have adversely affected welfare services and educational and Social Security benefits in the United States.
    a. protected classes.
    b. immigration.
    c. uniform guidelines.
    d. bona fide occupational qualifications.

LO 4 _____ 15. An important procedural document for managers that applies to employee selection procedures in the areas of hiring, retention, promotion, transfer, demotion, dismissal, and referral is
    a. affirmative action.
    b. employee leasing.
    c. *Uniform Guidelines*.
    d. sexual harassment rules.

LO 4 _____ 16. When using a test or other selection instrument to choose individuals for employment, employers must be able to prove
    a. affirmative action.
    b. adverse impact.
    c. disparate treatment.
    d. validity.

LO 5 _____ 17. For an applicant or employee to pursue a discrimination case successfully, the individual must establish that the employer's selection procedures resulted in a(n)
    a. adverse impact on a protected class.
    b. undue process.
    c. affirmative action claim.
    d. violation of human rights.

LO 5 _____   18. As a rule of thumb to determine adverse impact on enforcement
proceedings, the Equal Employment Opportunity Commission has
adopted
   a. affirmative action procedures.
   b. the four-fifths rule.
   c. minimal wage provisions.
   d. overtime provisions.

LO 5 _____   19. The act of purposeful discrimination by an employer is called
   a. disparate treatment.
   b. adverse impact.
   c. antidiscrimination.
   d. bona fide occupational qualifications.

LO 5 _____   20. *Griggs v Duke Power Co.* was concerned with a minority person
meeting the qualifications for a position as a coal handler and exposed
problems with
   a. sexual harassment.
   b. employment selection procedures.
   c. job burnout.
   d. employment fatigue.

LO 5 _____   21. The type of analysis that will classify protected-class members by
number and the type of job they hold within the organization is
   a. adverse impact.
   b. workforce utilization.
   c. business necessity.
   d. adverse treatment.

LO 5 _____   22. A benchmark case in which the Supreme Court established two
important principles—that discrimination need not be overt or
intentional and that employment practices must be job-related— was
   a. *Hopwood v State of Texas.*
   b. *Albermarle Paper Company v Moody.*
   c. *Wards Cove Packing Company v Antonio.*
   d. *Griggs v Duke Power Company.*

LO 5 _____   23. The commission that was created from Title VII of the Civil Rights Act
of 1964 was the
   a. Security Exchange Commission.
   b. Federal Trade Commission.
   c. Equal Employment Opportunity Commission.
   d. Business Necessity Commission.

LO 6 _____ 24. Employers of 100 or more employees (except state and local government employers) and government contractors and subcontractors subject to Executive Order 11286 must file annually a(n)
   a. Business Office Report.
   b. Human Resources Plan.
   c. Labor Office Hours Report.
   d. EEO-1 report (Employer Information Report).

LO 7 _____ 25. Employees who wish to file a charge of discrimination must do so within _____ of the alleged unlawful practice.
   a. 180 days
   b. 365 days
   c. two years
   d. five years

LO 7 _____ 26. Discrimination cases that are "dual-filed" involve
   a. both federal and state governments.
   b. two people with the same complaint.
   c. a repeat offense.
   d. a complaint by one person involving two incidents of discrimination.

LO 8 _____ 27. A policy that goes beyond equal employment opportunity by requiring organizations to comply with the law and correct past discriminatory practices by increasing the numbers of minorities and women in specific positions is
   a. human resources planning.
   b. job evaluation.
   e. performance appraisal.
   d. affirmative action.

LO 8 _____ 28. The following are reasons employers establish affirmative action programs, *except*
   a. provide an organizational profile that graphically illustrates their workforce demographics.
   b. establishing goals and timetables for employment of underutilized protected classes.
   c. monitor progress of the entire affirmative action program.
   d. develop a reactive strategy for recruitment and selection.

LO 8 _____ 29. The act of giving preference to members of protected classes to the extent that unprotected individuals believe they are suffering discrimination is
   a. reverse discrimination.
   b. job analysis.
   c. job evaluation.
   d. performance appraisal.

LO 8 _____   30. Equal employment opportunity legislation requires managers to provide
the same opportunities to
   a. customers and suppliers.
   b. all job applicants and employees regardless of ethnicity.
   c. business agents and labor unions.
   d. government agents and officials.

True/False

Identify the following statements as True or False.

Learning Outcome (LO)

LO 1 _____   1. Equal employment opportunity is a legal topic, however, it is not an
emotional issue.

LO 1 _____   2. Equal employment opportunity as a national priority has emerged slowly
in the United States.

LO 1 _____   3. The change in government and societal attitudes toward discrimination
was further prompted by decreasing public awareness of the economic
imbalance between nonwhites and whites.

LO 1 _____   4. Since as early as the nineteenth century, the public has not been
informed or aware of discriminatory employment practices in the United
States.

LO 2 _____   5. Laws have been passed barring discrimination pertaining to recruitment,
selection, performance appraisal, promotion, and compensation.

LO 2 _____   6. Employers violate the Equal Pay Act when differences in wages paid to
men and women for equal work are based on seniority systems, merit
considerations, or incentive pay plans.

LO 2 _____   7. Employers may defend their employment practices by a defense of bona
fide occupational qualifications and/or business necessity.

LO 2 _____   8. Title VII of the Civil Rights Act of 1991 requires employers to grant
complete religious freedom in employment situations.

LO 2 _____   9. The chances of age discrimination by employers are expected to increase
over time.

LO 2 _____ 10. Fair employment practices are state and local laws governing equal employment opportunity that are often less comprehensive than federal laws.

LO 3 _____ 11. Quid pro quo sexual harassment can occur when unwelcome sexual conduct has the purpose or effect of unreasonably interfering with job performance.

LO 3 _____ 12. In a hostile environment, sexual harassment can occur when submission to or rejection of sexual conduct is used as a basis for employment decisions.

LO 4 _____ 13. Employers are completely certain about the appropriateness of specific selection procedures, especially those related to testing and selection.

LO 4 _____ 14. Under the *Uniform Guidelines*, the use of any selection procedure that has an adverse impact on the hiring, promotion, or other employment or membership opportunities of members of any race, sex, or ethnic group is considered to be discriminatory.

LO 5 _____ 15. Adverse impact refers to the rejection for employment, placement, or promotion of a significantly lower percentage of a nonprotected class when compared with a protected class.

LO 5 _____ 16. An alternative to the population comparison rule, and one increasingly used in discrimination lawsuits, is to apply the 80/20 analysis to the observed applicant flow data.

LO 5 _____ 17. Hiring individuals who must meet a minimum height or appearance standard (at the expense of protected class members) is evidence of a restricted policy by an employer.

LO 5 _____ 18. The *Uniform Guidelines* have been given added importance through three leading Supreme Court cases; each case is noteworthy because it elaborates on the concepts of affirmative action, job enlargement, and job enrichment.

LO 5 _____ 19. Equal Employment Opportunity Commission guidelines are not federal mandates by administrative rules and regulations published in the *Federal Register*.

LO 6 _____ 20. Equal Employment Opportunity Commission has developed posters which employers are required to display in prominent places.

LO 7 _____   21.   Managers and supervisors must retaliate against individuals who invoke their legal rights to file charges or to support other employees during Equal Employment Opportunity Commission proceedings.

LO 7 _____   22.   Since managers and supervisors are key to preventing and correcting discrimination, they, in particular, must be trained to understand employee rights and managerial obligations.

LO 8 _____   23.   Affirmative action is achieved by having organizations follow specific guidelines and establish goals to ensure that they have a balanced and representative workforce.

LO 8 _____   24.   Affirmative action has consistently resulted in improvement of the employment status of protected groups.

LO 8 _____   25.   Since the beginning of the 1990s, federal courts have decreasingly restricted the use of race and ethnicity in awarding scholarships, determining college admissions, making layoff decisions, selecting employees, promoting employees, and awarding government contracts.

Matching

Match each term with the proper definition.

Terms

a.   adverse impact
b.   affirmative action
c.   bona fide occupational qualification (BFOQ)
d.   business necessity
e.   charge form
f.   chief diversity officer
g.   disabled individual
h.   disparate treatment
i.   EEO-1 report

j.   equal employment opportunity
k.   fair employment practices (FEPs)
l.   four-fifths rule
m.   protected classes
n.   reasonable accommodation
o.   reverse discrimination
p.   sexual harassment
q.   *Uniform Guidelines on Employee Selection Procedures*
r.   workforce utilization analysis

Definitions

_____ 1. any person who has a physical or mental impairment that substantially limits such person's major life activities.

_____ 2. act of giving preference to members of protected classes to the extent that unprotected individuals believe they are suffering discrimination.

_____ 3. the treatment of individuals in all aspects of employment—hiring, promotion, training, etc.— in a fair and nonbiased manner.

_____ 4. individuals of a minority race, women, older persons, and those with disabilities who are covered by federal laws on equal employment opportunity.

_____ 5. attempt by employers to adjust, without undue hardship, the working conditions or schedules of employees with disabilities or religious preferences.

_____ 6. state and local laws governing equal employment opportunity that are often more comprehensive than federal laws.

_____ 7. procedural document published in the _Federal Register_ to assist employers in complying with federal regulations against discriminatory actions.

_____ 8. a concept that refers to the rejection of a significantly higher percentage of a protected class for employment, placement, or promotion when compared with the successful, nonprotected class.

_____ 9. rule of thumb followed by the Equal Employment Opportunity Commission in determining adverse impact in enforcement proceedings.

_____ 10. process of classifying protected class members by number and by the type of job they hold within the organization.

_____ 11. situation in which protected-class members receive unequal treatment or are evaluated by different standards.

_____ 12. unwelcome advances, requests for sexual favors, and other verbal or physical conduct of a sexual nature in the working environment.

_____ 13. suitable defense against a discrimination charge only where age, religion, sex, or national origin is an actual qualification for performing the job.

_____ 14. work-related practice that is necessary for the safe and efficient operation of an organization.

_____ 15. an employer information report that must be filed annually by employers of 100 or more employees (except state and local government employers) and government contractors and subcontractors to determine an employer's workforce composition.

_____ 16. discrimination complaint filed with the Equal Employment Opportunity Commission by employees or job applicants.

_____ 17. policy that goes beyond equal employment opportunity by requiring organizations to comply with the law and to correct past discriminatory practices by increasing the numbers of minorities and women in specific positions.

_____ 18. a top executive responsible for implementing a firm's diversity efforts.

Internet Exercises

Examine the implications of the Supreme Court Decision in Smith v. City of Jackson for ADEA. http://digitalcommons.ilr.cornell.edu/cgi/viewcontent.cgi?article=1184&context=key_workplace

Why is workplace diversity prized in the business community? http://www.findarticles.com/p/articles/mi_m3495/is_9_48/ai_108315218/print.

How to Proceed with a Charge of Discrimination against an Employer

Assume you are a minority student from a protected class. How could you charge an employer with discrimination if you are a candidate and are denied employment for a job that has been advertised?

An individual may take a discrimination charge against an employer to the regional office of the Equal Employment Opportunity Commission or take the charge to the state Human Relations Commission.

An individual can bring forth a charge of adverse impact against an employer. This concept refers to the rejection of a significantly higher percentage of a protected class for employment, placement, or promotion when compared with the successful nonprotected class of individuals. An individual can charge an employer with disparate treatment, which is a situation in which protected-class members receive unequal treatment or are evaluated by different standards.

Individuals can bring forth a charge of the violation of the four-fifths rule against an employer, which is a rule of thumb followed by the Equal Employment Opportunity Commission in determining adverse impact for use in enforcement proceedings.

Any evidence that an employer has a selection procedure that excludes members of a protected class, whether intentional or not, constitutes adverse impact. Hiring individuals who must meet a minimum height or appearance standard (at the expense of protected class members) is evidence of such a restrictive policy.

Individuals who believe they have been unjustly rejected for employment may demonstrate disparate treatment through the McDonnell Douglas test.

SOLUTIONS

Multiple Choice:	True/False:	Matching:
1. a	1. False	1. g
2. a	2. True	2. o
3. c	3. False	3. j
4. b	4. False	4. m
5. d	5. True	5. n
6. b	6. False	6. k
7. d	7. True	7. q
8. c	8. False	8. a
9. b	9. True	9. l
10. b	10. False	10. r
11. b	11. False	11. h
12. a	12. False	12. p
13. c	13. False	13. c
14. b	14. True	14. d
15. c	15. False	15. i
16. d	16. False	16. e
17. a	17. True	17. b
18. b	18. False	18. f
19. a	19. False	
20. b	20. True	
21. b	21. False	
22. d	22. True	
23. c	23. True	
24. d	24. False	
25. a	25. False	
26. a		
27. d		
28. d		
29. a		
30. b		

False Statements Made True

1. Equal employment opportunity is **not only** a legal topic **but also an emotional issue**.

3. The change in government and societal attitudes toward discrimination was further prompted by **increasing** public awareness of the economic imbalance between nonwhites and whites.

4. Since as early as the nineteenth century, **the public has been aware** of discriminatory employment practices in the United States.

6. Employers **do not violate** the Equal Pay Act when differences in wages paid to men and women for equal work are based on seniority systems, merit considerations, or incentive pay plans.

8. Title VII of the Civil Rights Act of 1964 **does not** require employers to grant complete religious freedom in employment situations.

10. Fair employment practices are state and local laws governing equal employment opportunity that are often **more** comprehensive than federal laws.

11. Quid pro quo sexual harassment can occur when **submission to or rejection of sexual conduct is used as a basis for employment decisions.**

12. In a hostile environment, sexual harassment can occur when **unwelcome sexual conduct has the purpose or effect of unreasonably interfering with job performance or creating an intimidating, hostile, or offensive working environment.**

13. Employers are **often uncertain** about the appropriateness of specific selection procedures, especially those related to testing and selection.

15. Adverse impact refers to the rejection for employment, placement, or promotion of a significantly **higher** percentage of a **protected class** when compared with a **nonprotected class**.

16. An alternative to **the four-fifths rule**, and one increasingly used in discrimination lawsuits, is to apply the *standard deviation analysis* to the observed applicant flow data.

18. The *Uniform Guidelines* have been given added importance through three leading Supreme Court cases; each case is noteworthy because it elaborates on the concepts of **adverse impact, validity testing, and job relatedness.**

19. Equal Employment Opportunity Commission guidelines are not federal law **but administrative rules and regulations published in the *Federal Register*.**

21. Managers and supervisors **must not** retaliate against individuals who invoke their legal rights to file charges or to support other employees during Equal Employment Opportunity Commission proceedings.

24. Affirmative action **has not** consistently resulted in improvement of the employment status of protected groups.

25. **Since the mid-1990s**, federal courts have **increasingly** restricted the use of race and ethnicity in awarding scholarships, determining college admissions, making layoff decisions, selecting employees, promoting employees, and awarding government contracts.

CHAPTER 4

JOB ANALYSIS AND JOB DESIGN

In this chapter you will learn the relationship between job requirements and the performance of human resources management functions. You will learn that job requirements provide the foundation on which many human resources decisions, including those relating to recruitment, selection, training, evaluation, and compensation, must be based. It is essential that the requirements of each job in the organization are determined accurately. Supervisors and their employees must be aware of these job requirements. You will learn the relevance of job analysis and how it is used to write job descriptions and job specifications.

You will also understand the techniques used to maximize employee contributions, be able to discuss the various job characteristics that motivate employees, and, finally, explain how managers can implement alternative work schedules.

LEARNING OUTCOMES

After studying this chapter, you should be able to

LEARNING OUTCOME 1	Explain what a job analysis is, the parts that comprise it and how the information it generates is used in conjunction with a firm's HRM functions.
LEARNING OUTCOME 2	Explain how the data for a job analysis typically is collected.
LEARNING OUTCOME 3	Identify and explain the various sections of job descriptions.
LEARNING OUTCOME 4	Provide examples illustrating the various factors that must be taken into account when designing a job.

LEARNING OUTCOME 5	Discuss the various job characteristics that motivate employees.
LEARNING OUTCOME 6	Describe the different group techniques used to broaden a firm's job functions and maximize the contributions of employees.
LEARNING OUTCOME 7	Identify the different types of work schedules organizations are using today to motivate their employees.

CHAPTER SUMMARY RELATING TO LEARNING OUTCOMES

LEARNING OUTCOME A job analysis is the systematic process of collecting information about all of the parameters of a job—its basic responsibilities, the behaviors, skills, and the physical and mental requirements of the people who do it. A job analysis should also outline the tools needed to do the job, the environment and times at which it needs to done, with whom it needs to be done, and the outcome or performance level it should produce. The information a job analysis collects serves many HRM functions, including a firm's workflow and design of jobs, its legal compliance efforts, and the recruitment, selection, training and development, performance appraisal, and compensation of employees. To comply with the law, human resources decisions must be based on criteria objectively collected by analyzing the requirements of each job.

LEARNING OUTCOME 2 Job analysis data can be gathered in several ways—via interviews, questionnaires, observations, and diaries. Other more quantitative approaches include the U.S. Department of Labor's job analysis system, the Position Analysis Questionnaire system, the critical incident method, a task inventory analysis, and a competency-based analysis.

LEARNING OUTCOME 3 The format of job descriptions varies widely, often reflecting the needs of the organization and the expertise of the writer. At a minimum, job descriptions should contain a job title, a job identification section, and an essential functions section. A job specification section might also be included. Job descriptions should be written in clear and specific terms with consideration given to their legal implications.

LEARNING OUTCOME 4 Job design, which is an outgrowth of job analysis, focuses on restructuring jobs in order to capture the talents of employees, improve their work satisfaction, and an organization's performance. Four basic factors need to be taken into account when a job is designed: the organization's objectives; industrial engineering concerns of analyzing work methods and establishing time standards; ergonomic considerations; and behavioral aspects such as the motivation of employees.

46

`LEARNING OUTCOME 5`   In the job characteristics model, five job factors affect employees' satisfaction: job skill variety, task identity, task significance, autonomy, and feedback. All factors should be built into jobs, since each factor affects the psychological state of employees. Job enlargement, job enrichment, job rotation, employee empowerment, and job crafting are techniques that have been developed to address the motivation of employees.

`LEARNING OUTCOME 6`   Increasingly, firms are using employee teams to solve unique and complex problems, enhance the collaboration among workers, improve their morale and performance, and make the most of a firm's scarce resources. An employee team is a group of individuals working together toward a common purpose, in which members have complementary skills, members' work is mutually dependent, and the group has discretion over the tasks it performs. The types of teams commonly used are crossfunctional teams, project teams, self-directed teams, task-force teams, process-improvement teams, and virtual teams.

`LEARNING OUTCOME 7`   Flexible work schedules can be implemented by the organization or requested by individual employees. Employers sometimes depart from the traditional workday or workweek to improve their productivity and the morale of their employees by giving them more control over the hours they work. Compressed workweeks, flextime, job sharing, and telecommuting allow employees to adjust their work periods to accommodate their particular lifestyles.

REVIEW QUESTIONS

Multiple Choice

Choose the letter of the word or phrase that best completes each statement.

Learning Outcome (LO)

LO 1 _____   1. Normally a manager or an HR manager such as a _____ is responsible for collecting the information for a job analysis.
   a. job designer
   b. job creator
   c. job analyst
   d. job reporter

LO 1 _____   2. The process of obtaining information about jobs by determining their duties, tasks, or activities is known as
   a. job analysis
   b. job research.
   c. job intelligence.
   d. job design.

LO 1 _____ 3. A job specification is a statement
    a. as to the specific job that one desires.
    b. the specific job to be eliminated in organization being downsized.
    c. of the knowledge skills, and abilities of a person.
    d. of the tasks, duties, and responsibilities of a job.

LO 1 _____ 4. _____ is sometimes called the cornerstone of HRM.
    a. strategic HR planning
    b. training and development
    c. job design
    d. job analysis

LO 1 _____ 5. In the performance appraisal process, it is important to identify
    a. what pleases the specific boss..
    b. what non-job related criteria should be used.
    c. what constitutes good performance.
    d. what will please the employee.

LO 1 _____ 6. To assure legal compliance and avoid discrimination charges
    a. ensure that a job's duties match the job description.
    b. use job related criteria.
    c. both of the above.
    d. none of the above.

LO 2 _____ 7. The job analysis technique that is worker-oriented and covers 194 different tasks is
    a. task inventory development.
    b. the critical incident method.
    c. functional job analysis.
    d. the position analysis questionnaire.

LO 2 _____ 8. The job analysis technique that was pioneered by the US Air Force is
    a. task inventory development.
    b. the critical incident method.
    c. functional job analysis.
    d. the position analysis questionnaire.

LO 2 _____ 9. The job analysis technique that relies on building job profiles that look at the responsibility and activities of jobs and the worker competencies necessary to accomplish them is
    a. task inventory development.
    b. the critical incident method.
    c. the competency-based analysis.
    d. the position analysis questionnaire.

LO 3 _____   10. Most job descriptions contain all of the following *except*
a. job title.
b. job identification.
c. job duties section.
d. job evaluation section.

LO 3 _____   11. From the employer's standpoint, written _____ can minimize the misunderstandings that occur between managers and their subordinates concerning job requirements.
a. job specifications.
b. position analyses questionnaires.
c. job descriptions
d. critical incidences

LO 4 _____   12. Industrial engineering primarily involves
a. work methods and time standards.
b. ensuring physical well-being.
c. an outgrowth of job analysis.
d. None of the above.

LO 4 _____   13. Ergonomics primarily involves
a. work methods and time standards.
b. ensuring physical well-being.
c. an outgrowth of job analysis.
d. None of the above.

LO 4 _____   14. Which is one of the four elements of job design?
a. economic analysis.
b. behavioral concerns that influence an employee's job satisfaction.
c. mathematical modeling.
d. corporate social responsibility issues.

LO 4 _____   15. The term that describes the process that is concerned with structuring jobs in order to improve the organization's efficiency and employee satisfaction is
a. job specification.
b. job analysis.
c. job design.
d. job selection.

LO 4 _____   16. In order to capture the talents of employees while improving organization performance, job design is concerned with
a. modifying jobs.
b. changing jobs.
c. enriching jobs.
d. all of the above.

LO 4 _____ 17. Which are elements of job design?
  a. industrial engineering concerns.
  b. organizational objectives.
  c. both of the above.
  d. none of the above.

LO 5 _____ 18. Any effort that makes work more rewarding or satisfying by adding more meaningful tasks to an employee's job is
  a. job enlargement.
  b. job specification.
  c. job enrichment.
  d. job analysis.

LO 5 _____ 19. Herzberg's concept of fulfilling employee needs such as self-fulfillment and self-esteem while achieving long-term job satisfaction and performance goals is known as
  a. job enlargement.
  b. job specification.
  c. job enrichment.
  d. job analysis.

LO 5 _____ 20. The following are traits in the job characteristics model *except*
  a. skill variety.
  b. task identity.
  c. task significance.
  d. consensus decision making.

LO 5 _____ 21. A technique of involving employees in their work through the process of inclusion is
  a. employee empowerment.
  b. employee downsizing.
  c. job enlargement.
  d. reengineering of work.

LO 5 _____ 22. Which is not one of three psychological states involved in the job characteristics model?
  a. experiencing meaningfulness of the work performed.
  b. responsibility for work outcomes.
  c. the desire to innovate and create.
  d. knowledge of the results of the work performed.

LO 5 _____   23. _____ is a naturally occurring phenomenon whereby employees mold their tasks to fit their individual strengths, passions, and motives better.
a. dejobbing
b. employee engagement
c. job crafting
d. employee empowerment

LO 6 _____   24. _____ teams are often championed as the best form of team.
a. virtual
b. self-directed
c. cross-functional
d. project

LO 6 _____   25. Which of the following are not one of the characteristics identified with successful teams?
a. commitment of shared goals and objectives.
b. energetic team members.
c. a strong leader.
d. open communication.

LO 6 _____   26. Advanced computer and telecommunications technology to link team members who are geographically dispersed, often worldwide, are
a. employee involvement groups.
b. virtual teams.
c. job analysis.
d. flextime workers.

LO 7 _____   27. From the employer's standpoint, flextime can be most helpful in
a. predicting employee turnover.
b. recruiting and retaining personnel.
c. developing job sharing.
d. flexible and adaptable work schedules.

LO 7 _____   28. The arrangement whereby two part-time employees perform a job that otherwise would be held by one full-time employee is called
a. job sharing.
b. job rotation.
c. flextime.
d. flexible schedules.

LO 7 _____ 29. The following are disadvantages to flextime *except*
    a. It improves service to customers/clients by extending operating hours.
    b. It is not suited for some jobs.
    c. It creates communications problems for managers and employees.
    d. Managers may have to extend their workweek.

LO 7 _____ 30. Use of personal computers and communication technology to do work at home that is traditionally done in the workplace is called
    a. job sharing.
    b. job rotation.
    c. flextime.
    d. telecommuting.

True/False

Identify the following statements as True or False.

Learning Outcome (LO)

LO 1 _____ 1. A job analyst is an HR manager.

LO 1 _____ 2. A job specification outlines in detail the specific KSAOs required of the person performing the job.

LO 1 _____ 3. A job analysis cannot be done until Strategic HR Planning is complete.

LO 1 _____ 4. Job analysis is the process of obtaining information about jobs by determining what the duties, tasks, or activities of those jobs are.

LO 1 _____ 5. Job descriptions and job specifications are no longer of value to those who make human resources management (HRM) decisions because in today's world jobs are constantly changing.

LO 2 _____ 6. Common methods of analyzing jobs when undertaking job analysis would include interviews, questionnaires, observation, and diaries.

LO 2 _____ 7. The task inventory method can be considered a job-oriented type of job analysis.

LO 2 _____ 8. The objective of the critical incident method of job analysis is to identify 194 items in the checklist of the position analysis questionnaire.

LO 3 _____ 9. In writing a job description, selection of a job title is important in providing status to the employee; for example, "sanitation engineer" is preferable to "garbage collector."

LO 3 _____ 10. Skills that are irrelevant to a job include education, social interaction, specialized training, personal traits or abilities, and family dexterities.

LO 3 _____ 11. If you work for a firm that still uses job descriptions, remember that continual change requires flexibility and thus HR no longer includes a job duties section.

LO 4 _____ 12. There are two job design methods—job enrichment and job characteristics—which seek to incorporate the behavioral needs of employees as they perform their individual jobs.

LO 4 _____ 13. Job enlargement, or the vertical expansion of jobs, may be accomplished by increasing the autonomy and responsibility of employees.

LO 5 _____ 14. According to Richard Hackman and Greg Oldham, their job characteristics model proposes that three psychological states of a jobholder result in improved work performance, internal motivation, and lower absenteeism and turnover.

LO 5 _____ 15. Empowerment encourages employees to become innovators and managers of their own work, and it involves them in their jobs in ways that give them more control and autonomous decision-making capabilities.

LO 5 _____ 16. The outgrowth of scientific management was industrial engineering, which is concerned with analyzing work methods and establishing time standards.

LO 5 _____ 17. Ergonomics is concerned with equipment design and must only take into consideration the mental ability of operators to use the equipment and to react through vision, hearing, and touch to the information the equipment conveys.

LO 5 _____ 18. Ergonomics has recently focused on the increase and inclusion of many repetitive motion injuries, particularly those related to the back and wrist.

LO 6 _____ 19. Designing work to enhance group or worker productivity includes the techniques of collaboration and synergy.

LO 6 _____ 20. Permanent groups of five to ten employees doing similar or related work who meet together regularly to identify, analyze, and suggest solutions to shared problems are often referred to as task forces.

LO 6 _____ 21. Job enrichment occurs when the interactions and outcomes of team members are greater than the sum of their individual efforts.

LO 6 _____ 22. Work teams can operate in a variety of organization structures, each with different strategic purposes or functional activities.

LO 7 _____ 23. Flextime, or flexible working hours, permits employees the option of choosing daily starting and quitting times, provided they work a certain number of hours per day or week.

LO 7 _____ 24. Telecommuting is the use of personal computers, networks, and other communications technology such as fax machines to do work in the home that is traditionally done in the workplace.

LO 7 _____ 25. A variant of telecommuting is the cyber workspace where employees are in the office selling to, or servicing, customers or are stationed at other remote locations working as if they were in the field.

Matching

Match each term with the proper definition.

Terms

a. critical incident method
b. dejobbing
c. employee empowerment
d. employee teams
e. ergonomics
f. flextime
g. industrial engineering
h. job
i. job analysis
j. job characteristics model

k. job crafting
l. job description
m. job design
n. job enlargement
o. job enrichment
p. job rotation
q. job specification
r. position analysis questionnaire (PAQ)
s. task inventory analysis
t. telecommuting
u. virtual team

Definitions

_____ 1. flexible working hours that give employees the option of choosing daily starting and quitting times, provided that they work a set number of hours per day or week.

_____ 2. empowerment approach that purports that improving the psychological state of a jobholder results in improved work performance, internal motivation, and lower absenteeism and turnover.

_____ 3. statement of the needed knowledge, skills, and abilities of the person who is to perform the job.

_____ 4. a naturally occurring phenomenon whereby employees mold their tasks to fit their individual strengths, passions, and motives better.

_____ 5. granting employees power to initiate change, thereby encouraging them to take charge of what they do.

_____ 6. use of personal computers, networks, and other communications technology to do work in the home that has traditionally been done in the workplace.

_____ 7. outgrowth of job analysis that improves jobs and is concerned with structuring jobs in order to improve organization efficiency and employee job satisfaction.

_____ 8. a field of study concerned with analyzing work methods and establishing time standards.

_____ 9. logical outgrowth of employee involvement and the philosophy of empowerment.

_____ 10. an interdisciplinary approach to designing equipment and systems that can be easily and efficiently used by employees.

_____ 11. the process of adding a greater variety of tasks to a job.

_____ 12. job analysis method in which important job tasks are identified for job success.

_____ 13. process of obtaining information about a job by determining the job's duties, tasks, or activities.

_____ 14. enhancing a job by adding more meaningful tasks and duties to make the work more rewarding or satisfying.

_____ 15. a team with widely dispersed members linked through computer and telecommunications technology.

55

_____ 16. questionnaire covering 194 different tasks which, by means of a five-point scale, seeks to determine the degree to which different tasks are involved in performing a particular job.

_____ 17. a group of related activities and duties.

_____ 18. refers to a process of structuring organizations not around jobs but around projects that are constantly changing.

_____ 19. statement of a job's tasks, duties, and responsibilities.

_____ 20. an organized list of tasks and their descriptions used as a basis to identify components of different jobs.

_____ 21. a process whereby employees rotate in and out of different jobs.

Internet Exercises

What alternative work arrangements are used by an employer?
http://careerplanning.about.com/cs/flextime/a/flextime.htm.

How is job analysis used as an employment tool?
http://www.ucp.org/ucp_channeldoc.cfm/1/17/11928/11928-11928/4605

How to Request a Realistic Job Preview

A job applicant may request a realistic job preview when interviewing with an employer or the Human Resources Department.

A line manager or the Human Resources Department should provide a realistic job preview in every interview. This process is an accurate portrayal of the job that the applicant is expected to perform. It would include the job title, duties and responsibilities, and the authority delegated in the performance of a job. Opportunities for growth and a career development program should be discussed to provide the greatest amount of information to each job applicant. Remember, it is the responsibility of the individual applying for a job or the employee to initiate the discussion of a career development program. One can also ask to see a job specification, which outlines the minimal qualifications required for a job. A job specification specifies the abilities and skills required to perform a job. It includes the educational requirements and work experiences necessary. An applicant should attempt to match these job requirements to his or her own strengths.

SOLUTIONS

Multiple Choice:	True/False:	Matching:
1. c	1. True	1. f
2. a	2. True	2. j
3. c	3. False	3. q
4. d	4. True	4. k
5. c	5. False	5. c
6. c	6. True	6. t
7. d	7. True	7. m
8. a	8. False	8. g
9. c	9. True	9. d
10. d	10. False	10. e
11. c	11. False	11. n
12. a	12. True	12. a
13. b	13. False	13. i
14. b	14. True	14. o
15. c	15. True	15. u
16. d	16. True	16. r
17. c	17. False	17. h
18. c	18. False	18. b
19. c	19. True	19 l
20. d	20. False	20. s
21. a	21. False	21. p
22. c	22. True	
23. c	23. True	
24. b	24. True	
25. c	25. False	
26. b		
27. b		
28. a		
29. a		
30. d		

False Statements Made True

3. A job analysis **is used for** Strategic HR Planning.

5. Job descriptions and job specifications **are** of value to those who make human resources management (HRM) decisions.

8. The objective of the critical incident method of job analysis is to **identify critical job tasks**.

10. Skills that are **relevant** to a job include education or **experience**, specialized training, personal traits or abilities, and **manual** dexterities.

11. If you work for a firm that uses job descriptions, remember that HR includes a job duties section.

13. Job **enrichment**, or the vertical expansion of jobs, may be accomplished by increasing the autonomy and responsibility of employees.

17. Ergonomics **attempts to accommodate the human capabilities and limitations of those who are to perform a job. It is concerned with adapting the entire job system—the work, the work environment, the machine and equipment, and the processes—to match human characteristics**.

18. Ergonomics has recently focused on the **elimination, or at least the reduction**, of many repetitive motion injuries, particularly those related to the back and wrist.

20. Permanent groups of five to ten employees doing similar or related work who meet together regularly to identify, analyze, and suggest solutions to shared problems are often referred to as **employee involvement groups**.

21. **Synergy** occurs when the interactions and outcomes of team members are greater than the sum of their individual efforts.

25. A variant of telecommuting is the **virtual office** where employees are in the **field** selling to, or servicing, customers or are stationed at other remote locations working as if they were in the **home office**.

CHAPTER 5

EXPANDING THE TALENT POOL: RECRUITMENT AND CAREERS

In this chapter you will learn about multiple approaches to the recruiting process. Employers use internal promotion and transfer to fill as many positions as possible above the entry level. You will learn the relevance of career planning throughout your tenure of employment. It is important to understand that top management must support career development. You will understand the knowledge and skills needed to perform individual jobs. You will learn how assessment centers are used in the recruiting process. Finally, you will learn the advantages of belonging to a women's network.

LEARNING OUTCOMES

After studying this chapter, you should be able to

LEARNING OUTCOME 1	Describe how a firm's strategy affects its recruiting efforts.
LEARNING OUTCOME 2	Outline the methods by which firm's recruit internally.
LEARNING OUTCOME 3	Outline the methods by which firm's recruit externally.
LEARNING OUTCOME 4	Explain the techniques organizations can use to improve their recruiting efforts.
LEARNING OUTCOME 5	Explain how career management programs integrate the needs of individual employees and their organizations.
LEARNING OUTCOME 6	Explain why diverse recruitment and career development activities are important to companies.

CHAPTER SUMMARY RELATING TO LEARNING OUTCOMES

LEARNING OUTCOME To expand the talent pool of organizations—the number and kind of people available for employment—organizations must focus on multiple approaches to recruitment and career management. Which internal and outside sources and methods are used in recruiting will depend on the strategy and goals of the organization, conditions of the labor market, and specifications of the jobs to be filled.

LEARNING OUTCOME 2 Employers usually find it advantageous to use internal promotions and transfers to fill as many openings as possible above the entry level. By recruiting from within, an organization can capitalize on the previous investments they have made in recruiting, selecting, training, and developing its current employees and rewarding them. Internal job postings, performance appraisals, skills inventories, replacement charts, and assessment centers are ways in which firms identify internal talent.

LEARNING OUTCOME 3 Outside candidates are recruited when internal talent is lacking or a firm wants to hire employees with expertise from other organizations for competitive reasons and to prevent the inbreeding of ideas within their organization. To help meet a firm's EEO requirement and diversify its talent pools, firms also look externally for candidates. Advertisements, the Internet, social networks, mobile recruiting, employment agencies, tapping educational institutions and professional associations, and rerecruiting are among the many ways firms recruit external candidates.

LEARNING OUTCOME HR managers have many tools available to them to gauge their efforts and improve their recruiting. Using realistic job reviews, surveying managers and applicants about the process, and examining metrics such as the cost per hire, time to fill a position, and yield ratios are some of the ways in which firms evaluate their recruiting efforts. An applicant tracking system (ATS) can help a firm automatically track and calculate many of these statistics.

LEARNING OUTCOME 5 Identifying and developing talent is a responsibility of all managers. A career development program is a dynamic process that should integrate the career goals of employees with the goals of the organization. Job opportunities can be identified by studying jobs and determining the knowledge and skills each one requires. Once that is accomplished, key jobs can be identified, and job progressions can be planned. These progressions can then serve as a basis for developing the career paths of employees. Employees need to be made aware of the organization's philosophy and its goals; otherwise they will not know how their goals match those of the organization. Mentoring has been found to be valuable for providing guidance and support to employees and potential managers.

LEARNING OUTCOME 6 The first step toward facilitating the career development of women is to eliminate barriers to their advancement. Creating women's networks, providing special training for women, accepting women as valued members of the organization, providing mentors for them, and accommodating families have been found to be effective ways to facilitate women's career development.

A diversified workforce is composed of many different groups, an important segment of which is minority groups. Many organizations have special programs such as internships that provide minority groups with hands-on experience as well as special training opportunities. Other groups that require the attention of management are the disabled, older workers, and dual career couples, who often need flexible working options.

REVIEW QUESTIONS

Multiple Choice

Choose the letter of the word or phrase that best completes each statement.

Learning Outcome (LO)

LO 1 _____   1. RPO is the practice of _____ an organizations recruiting function.
   a. resourcing
   b. insourcing
   c. outsourcing
   d. global sourcing

LO 1 _____   2. Recruting potential employees internationally is known as
   a. resourcing.
   b. insourcing.
   c. outsourcing.
   d. global sourcing.

LO 1 _____   3. An example of an _____ would be a firm in which those at higher organizational levels all started out at entry level.
   a. exemplary firm
   b. internal labor market
   c. progressive labor market
   d. none of the above

LO 2 _____   4. A 9-box grid is
   a. an experimental tool in HR techology.
   b. a way to see both actual and potential performance.
   c. often used by HR managers in the container industry.
   d. none of the above.

LO 2 _____ 5. One study has shown that in hiring decisions, managers tend to
_____ unfamiliar candidates and _____ known ones.
   a. undervalue, overvalue
   b. overvalue, undervalue
   c. undervalue, undervalue
   d. overvalue, overvalue

LO 3 _____ 6. One of the most common methods of attracting applicants is through
   a. advertisements.
   b. referrals.
   c. friendship.
   d. billboards..

LO 3 _____ 7. The most commonly used search tactic by job seekers is the
   a. radio.
   b. internet.
   c. billboard.
   d. transportation service.

LO 3 _____ 8. Most job positions are filled through
   a. word-of-mouth recommendations.
   b. television ads.
   c. billboard ads.
   d. radio ads.

LO 3 _____ 9. The practice of hiring relatives is referred to as
   a. brotherhood.
   b. fraternal care.
   c. nepotism.
   d. sisterhood.

LO 3 _____ 10. A good source of young applicants with formal training but with
relatively little full-time experience is
   a. television.
   b. radio.
   c. billboard advertisements.
   d. educational institutions.

LO 3 _____ 11. A principle source of applicants for blue-collar and some professional
jobs is
   a. labor unions.
   b. educational institutions.
   c. television ads.
   d. billboard advertisements.

LO 3 _____   12. Companies that place their employees with subscribers on a permanent
basis are
a. employee-leasing firms.
b. educational services.
c. labor unions.
d. billboards.

LO 3 _____   13. According to the Society for Human Resource Management , companies
with fewer than 50 employees can save from $5000 to $50,000 in time
an labor costs annually
a. by hiring a PEO.
b. by reducing labor turnover.
c. by offshoring.
d. through realistic job previews (RJP).

LO 4 _____   14. The percentage of applicants from a particular source that make it to the
next stage in the selection process is called a
a. labor utility.
b. yield ratio.
c. recruiter.
d. labor-to-hour ratio.

LO 4 _____   15. Applicants are informed about all aspects of the job, including both its
desirable and undesirable facets, with a
a. selection device.
b. labor turnover.
c. test.
d. realistic job preview (RJP).

LO 4 _____   16. Time to fill refers to
a. how long it takes to fill a job opening.
b. the appropriate time that a job opening must be filled.
c. the time to begin recruiting for an expansion of the firm.
d. none of the above.

LO 4 _____   17. Yield ratios are used to evaluate
a. sources of applicants.
b. applicants.
c. the profit resulting from recruiting.
d. all of the above.

LO 4 _____ 18. An Applicant Tracking System is used by recruiters to
a. post job openings.
b. track costs.
c. contact potential candidates.
d. all of the above.

LO 5 _____ 19. Lines of advancement for individuals in an occupational field within an organization are
a. employee cards.
b. career paths.
c. application turnovers.
d. career plans.

LO 5 _____ 20. The career stage which often lasts until age 25 is known as
a. preparation for work.
b. organizational entry.
c. early career.
d. midcareer.

LO 5 _____ 21. The placement of an employee in another job for which the duties, responsibilities, status, and remuneration are approximately equal to those of the previous job is a
a. transfer.
b. promotion.
c. demotion.
d. bumping procedure.

LO 5 _____ 22. Relocation services include all of the following *except*
a. moving expenses.
b. spouse transfer.
c. cultural orientation.
d. language training.

LO 5 _____ 23. Organizations provide job-finding help for terminated employees through
a. recruitment.
b. selection.
c. retraining.
d. outplacement services.

LO 5 _____   24. A situation in which, either for organizational or personal reasons, the
probability of moving up the career ladder is low is called a
a. career plan.
b. promotion.
c. career plateau.
d. demotion.

LO 5 _____   25. A plateau that marks the end of possible promotions, meaning an
employee will have to leave the organization to find new opportunities
and challenges, is termed
a. career planning.
b. structural plateauing.
c. career developing.
d. career paths.

LO 5 _____   26. Executives and managers who coach, advise, and encourage employees
of lesser rank are called
a. managers.
b. executives.
c. mentors.
d. trainees.

LO 6 _____   27. The largest protected class is
a. women.
b. men.
c. trainees.
d. senior managers.

LO 6 _____   28. The most frequently cited advantage of employing people with
disabilities is
a. their superior attendance.
b. their loyalty.
c. the low turnover rate.
d. all of the above.

LO 6 _____   29. The most frequent organizational accommodation to dual-career couples
is/are
a. flextime.
b. street time.
c. promotion.
d. flexible working schedules.

LO 6 _____ 30. The major problem faced by dual-career couples is
   a. flextime.
   b. threat of relocation.
   c. promotion.
   d. flexible working schedules.

TRUE/FALSE

Identify the following statements as True or False.

Learning Outcome (LO)

LO 1 _____ 1. Firms need to avoid continually refining their recruiting efforts.

LO 1 _____ 2. Recruiters are often the reason why applicants select a given organization.

LO 1 _____ 3. In a period of high unemployment, there may be industries in which it is difficult to find qualified new workers.

LO 2 _____ 4. Performance appraisal is based on the past and identify talent for promotion.

LO 2 _____ 5. Replacement charts are an important tool for succession planning.

LO 2 _____ 6. When experienced employees leave an organization they are easy to replace because their years of experience are no longer technologically relevant.

LO 3 _____ 7. During periods of low unemployment, organizations may be able to maintain an adequate supply of qualified applicants from unsolicited résumés alone.

LO 3 _____ 8. In general, applicants who find employment through referral by a current employee tend to remain with the organization longer.

LO 3 _____ 9. Formal recruiting sources may yield higher selection rates than informal sources.

LO 3 _____ 10. The preparation of recruiting advertisements is time consuming and requires creativity in developing design and message content.

LO 3 _____ 11. If there is no possibility of employment in the organization at present or in the future, the applicant should be tactfully and frankly informed of this fact.

LO 3 _____ 12. Managers have found that the quality of employee-referred applicants is normally quite low since employees are generally hesitant to recommend individuals.

LO 3 _____ 13. One of the best ways to publicize a referral program is to celebrate successes.

LO 3 _____ 14. New data suggest that CEOs who are promoted from within their organizations actually outperform those hired from the outside.

LO 3 _____ 15. Increasingly, temps are being employed to fill positions once staffed by permanent employees because temporaries can be laid off quickly, and with less cost, when work lessens.

LO 5 _____ 16. Because having a successful career involves creating your own career path, it is up to each individual to identify his or her own knowledge, skills, abilities, interests, and values and seek out information about career options in order to set goals and develop career plans.

LO 5 _____ 17. One of the most important indicators of management support comes in the form of mentoring.

LO 5 _____ 18. The three principal criteria for determining promotions are merit, seniority, and personality.

LO 5 _____ 19. Individuals pursuing boundaryless careers develop their knowledge in ways specific to a given firm.

LO 5 _____ 20. Career counseling involves talking with employees about their current job activities and performance, their personal and career interests and goals, their personal skills, and suitable career development objectives.

LO 5 _____ 21. A fast-track program may provide for a relatively rapid progression—lateral transfers or promotions—through a number of managerial positions requiring exposure to different organizational functions.

LO 5 _____ 22. As a complement to mentoring, where relationships are more selective, networking relationships tend to be more varied and temporary.

LO 6 _____ 23. Today three out of five college graduates are women.

LO 6 _____ 24. Organizations are increasingly conducting their own glass ceiling audits.

LO 6 _____ 25. In recent years, black men have risen more rapidly than black women in corporate America.

Matching

Match each term with the proper definition.

Terms

a.	applicant tracking system	n.	job progressions
b.	branding	o.	mentors
c.	assessment center	p.	nepotism
d.	career counseling	q.	9-box grid
e.	career networking	r.	outplacement services
f.	career paths	s.	passive job seeker
g.	career plateau	t.	promotion
h.	dual-career partnerships	u.	recruiting process outsourcing (RPO)
i.	employee leasing	v.	realistic job preview (RJP)
j.	employee profile	w.	relocation services
k.	fast-track program	x.	rerecruiting
l.	global sourcing	y.	sabbatical
m.	internal labor market	z.	transfer
		a.a.	yield ratio

Definitions

_____ 1. a software application recruiters use to post job openings, screen resumes, and contact via e-mail potential candidates for interviews, and track the time and costs related to hiring people.

_____ 2. a preference for hiring relatives of current employees.

_____ 3. process of dismissing employees who are then hired by a leasing company (which handles all HR-related activities) and contracting with that company to lease back the employees.

_____   4. percentage of applicants from a recruitment source that make it to the next stage of the selection process.

_____   5. informing applicants about all aspects of the job, including both its desirable and undesirable facets.

_____   6. hierarchy of jobs a new employee might experience, ranging from a starting job to jobs that successively require more knowledge and/or skill.

_____   7. lines of advancement in an occupational field within an organization.

_____   8. change of assignment to a job at a higher level in the organization.

_____   9. placement of an individual in another job for which the duties, responsibilities, status, and remuneration are approximately equal to those of the previous job.

_____   10. services provided to an employee who is transferred to a new location, which might include help in moving, in selling a home, in orienting to a new culture, and/or in learning a new language.

_____   11. services provided by organizations to help terminated employees find a new job.

_____   12. process by which individuals are evaluated as they participate in a series of situations that resemble what they might be called upon to handle on the job.

_____   13. process of discussing with employees their current job activities and performance, their personal and career interests and goals, their personal skills, and suitable career development objectives.

_____   14. program that encourages young managers with high potential to remain with an organization by enabling them to advance more rapidly than those with less potential.

_____   15. executives who coach, advise, and encourage individuals of lesser rank.

_____   16. couples in which both members follow their own careers and actively support each other's career development.

_____   17. situation in which for either organizational or personal reasons the probability of moving up the career ladder is low.

_____   18. process of establishing mutually beneficial relationships with other business people, including potential clients and customers.

_____ 19. a company's efforts to help existing and prospective workers understand why it is a desirable place to work.

_____ 20. a profile of a worker developed by studying an organization's top performers in order to recruit similar types of people.

_____ 21. the business practice of searching for and utilizing goods sources from around the world.

_____ 22. labor markets in which workers are hired into entry level jobs and higher levels are filled from within.

_____ 23. people who are not looking for jobs but could be persuaded to take new ones given the right opportunity.

_____ 24. the practice of outsourcing an organization's recruiting function to an outside firm.

_____ 25. the process of keeping track of and maintaining relationships with former employees to see if they would be willing to return to the firm.

_____ 26. an extended period of time in which an employee leaves an organization to pursue other activities and later returns to his or her job.

Internet Exercises

What are some of the current policy provisions of relocation services for employees?
http://www.fpd.finop.umn.edu/groups/ppd/documents/policy/Moving.cfm.

Is there hope for dual-career couples to find satisfaction in all aspects of their lives?
http://physics.wm.edu/dualcareer.html.

How to Form an Effective Mentoring Relationship

In forming an effective mentoring relationship, you should:

1. Research the person's background.
2. Have someone introduce you or get involved with your mentor in a business setting.
3. Let your mentor know you admire him or her.
4. Keep in mind that mentoring is a two-way exchange.
5. Arrange a meeting and set goals, listen attentively, and ask questions.
6. Follow up, try the suggestions, and share the results.
7. Request an ongoing relationship by meeting on a regular basis.

SOLUTIONS

Multiple Choice:	True/False	Matching:
1. c	1. False	1. a
2. d	2. True	2. p
3. b	3. True	3. i
4. b	4. False	4. a.a.
5. b	5. True	5. v
6. a	6. False	6. n
7. b	7. False	7. f
8. a	8. True	8. t
9. c	9. False	9. z
10. d	10. True	10. w
11. a	11. True	11. r
12. a	12. False	12. c
13. a	13. True	13. d
14. b	14. True	14. k
15. d	15. True	15. o
16. a	16. True	16. h
17. a	17. True	17. g
18. d	18. False	18. e
19. b	19. False	19. b
20. a	20. True	20. j
21. a	21. True	21. l
22. b	22. True	22. m
23. d	23. True	23. s
24. c	24. True	24. u
25. b	25. False	25. x
26. c		26. y
27. a		
28. d		
29. d		
30. b		

False Statements Made True

1. Performance appraisal can identify talent for promotion.

4. Performance appraisal is **used to** identify talent for promotion.

6. When experienced employees leave an organization they are **not** easy to replace because **of** their years of experience.

7. During periods of high unemployment, organizations may be able to maintain an adequate supply of qualified applicants from unsolicited resumes alone.

9. Informal recruiting sources may yield higher selection rates than formal sources.

12. Managers have found that the quality of employee-referred applicants is normally quite high since employees are generally hesitant to recommend individuals.

18. The three principal criteria for determining promotions are merit, seniority, and potential.

19. Individuals pursuing more traditional careers develop their knowledge in ways specific to a given firm.

25. In recent years, black women have risen more rapidly than black men in corporate America.

CHAPTER 6

EMPLOYEE SELECTION

This chapter emphasizes the importance of personnel selection in the building of a productive workforce. Determining the qualifications of job candidates requires that as much information as possible be obtained from the candidates and other sources. Such information should be relevant to the job and sufficiently reliable and valid. It is essential that interviewers are thoroughly trained in how to obtain the information needed and how to avoid being discriminatory. Human resources practitioners need to understand job requirements in order to evaluate application forms, employment tests, interviews, and reference checks of individual candidates.

LEARNING OUTCOMES

After studying this chapter, you should be able to

LEARNING OUTCOME 1 Explain the objectives of the personnel selection process.

LEARNING OUTCOME 2 Explain what is required for an employee selection tool to be reliable and valid.

LEARNING OUTCOME 3 Illustrate the different approaches to conducting an employment interview.

LEARNING OUTCOME 4 Compare the value of different types of employment tests.

LEARNING OUTCOME 5 Describe the various decision strategies for selection.

CHAPTER SUMMARY RELATING TO LEARNING OUTCOMES

LEARNING OUTCOME   Selection is the process of choosing individuals who have relevant qualifications to fill existing or projected job openings. The selection process should start with a job analysis. Research shows that complete and clear job specifications help interviewers differentiate between qualified and unqualified applicants and reduces the effect of an interviewer's biases and prejudices. The number of steps in the selection process and their sequence will vary, not only with the organization, but also with the type and level of jobs to be filled.

LEARNING OUTCOME 2   The employee selection process should provide as much reliable and valid information as possible about applicants so that their qualifications can be carefully matched with the job's specifications. The information that is obtained should be clearly job-related or predict success on the job and free from potential discrimination. Reliability refers to the consistency of test scores over time and across measures. Validity refers to the accuracy of the measurements taken. Validity can be assessed in terms of whether the measurement is based on a job specification (content validity), whether test scores correlate with performance criteria (predictive validity), and whether the test accurately measures what it purports to measure (construct validity).

LEARNING OUTCOME 3   Interviews are customarily used in conjunction with résumés, application forms, biographical information blanks, references, background investigations, and various types of pre-employment tests. Despite problems with its validity, the employment interview remains central to the selection process. Depending on the type of job, applicants could be interviewed by one person, members of a work team, or other individuals in the organization. Structured interviews have been found to be better predictors of the performance of job applicants than non-structured interviews. Some interviews are situational and can focus on hypothetical situations or actual behavioral descriptions of a candidate's previous work experiences. Regardless of the technique chosen, those who conduct interviews should receive special training to acquaint them with interviewing methods and EEO considerations. The training should also make them more aware of the nature of the job and its requirements.

LEARNING OUTCOME 4   Pre-employment tests are more objective than interviews and can give managers a fuller sense of the capabilities of different candidates. A wide range of tests exists. Cognitive ability tests are especially valuable for assessing verbal, quantitative, and reasoning abilities. Personality and interest tests are perhaps best used for placement or career development. Job knowledge and work sample tests are achievement tests that are useful for determining whether a candidate can perform the duties of the job without further training. Physical ability tests can be used to prevent accidents and injuries, particularly for physically demanding work. However, they must not be used if they have a disparate impact on candidates in protected classes. Medical examinations and drug tests can only be legally administered after a conditional offer of employment has been made.

LEARNING OUTCOME 5   In the process of making decisions, all "can-do" and "will-do" factors should be assembled and weighted systematically so that the final decision can be based on a composite of the most reliable and valid information. Although the clinical approach to decision-making is used more than the statistical approach, the former lacks the accuracy of the latter. Compensatory models allow a candidate's high score on one predictor to make up for a low score on another. When the multiple cutoff model is used, only those candidates who score above a minimum cutoff level remain in the running. A variation of the multiple cutoff is the multiple hurdle model, which involves several stages and cutoff levels. Whichever of these approaches is used, the goal is to select a greater proportion of individuals who will be successful on the job.

REVIEW QUESTIONS

Multiple Choice

Choose the letter of the word or phrase that best completes each statement.

Learning Outcome (LO)

LO 1 _____   1. The cost of hiring an unsuccessful applicant includes
   a. direct costs.
   b. indirect costs.
   c. opportunity costs.
   d. all of the above.

LO 1 _____   2. Job specifications help identify the _____ employees need for success.
   a. physical appearance
   b. ancestry
   c. individual competencies
   d. beliefs

LO 1 _____   3. HR interviewers need to be familiar with
   a. the actual jobs, not just the interview process.
   b. the extent to which they can bend the rules.
   c. ways of making sure that what they ask or say is not recorded.
   d. none of the above.

LO 1 _____   4. The steps in the selection process
   a. are the same for everyone.
   b. vary according to the type of job.
   c. must all be followed even if the applicant is found to be unsatisfactory in the first step.
   d. a and c above.

LO 1 _____   5. In 2009 – 2010, internal promotions
       a. were more than half of all positions filled.
       b. increased from 34% in 2007.
       c. both of the above.
       d. none of the above.

LO 2 _____   6. The degree to which selection procedures yield comparable data over time is referred to as
       a. validity.
       b. reliability.
       c. both of the above.
       d. none of the above.

LO 2 _____   7. The degree to which selection a procedure measures a person's attributes is referred to as.
       a. validity.
       b. reliability.
       c. both of the above.
       d. none of the above.

LO 2 _____   8. Consistency refers to all of the following except
       a. two methods yield similar results.
       b. two or more raters are in agreement.
       c. the results of test and the results of a person's performance will always be the same.
       d. one has similar scores when a test is taken a few days apart.

LO 2 _____   9. A measurement procedure should be validated because validity
       a. is directly related to increases in employee productivity.
       b. is required by EEO regulations.
       c. both of the above.
       d. none of the above.

LO 2 _____   10. Cover letters and résumés are of value in
       a. determining who can be eliminated.
       b. providing objective information.
       c. providing consistently applied standards for their use.
       d. eliminating the use of irrelevant standards.

LO 2 _____   11. Concerns about résumé writing software include
       a. the need for applicants to use key words to be successful
       b. capable people may be rejected before a person ever sees their credentials.
       c. both of the above.
       d. use of the software is a problem for the technically challenged.

LO 2 _____   12. The benefit of video résumés includes all of the following except
     a. it provides information beyond the written information provided by applicants.
     b. people may be screened based on their looks rather than their qualifications.
     c. it shows employers how well applicants can present themselves.
     d. it provides interviewers a "preview" of the applicant.

LO 2 _____   13. An example of something that should not be on an application form would be
     a. the right to check reference checks.
     b. required employment testing.
     c. the applicant's marital status.
     d. warnings about information falsification.

LO 3 _____   14. Which are true of job interviews?
     a. interviews have problems with validity.
     b. interviews are central to the selection process.
     c. both of the above.
     d. none of the above.

LO 3 _____   15. Interviews that are situational focus on
     a. hypothetical situations.
     b. actual behavioral descriptions of previous experience.
     c. both of the above.
     d. none of the above.

LO 3 _____   16. A _____ interview is likely to begin with a broad open-ended question.
     a. nondirective
     b. structured
     c. situational
     d. behavioral description

LO 3 _____   17. A _____ interview involves about what the applicant actually did.
     a. nondirective
     b. structured
     c. situational
     d. behavioral description

LO 3 _____   18. A _____ interview involves asking the applicant about a hypothetical situation.
     a. nondirective
     b. structured
     c. situational
     d. behavioral description

LO 3 _____ 19. A _____ interview uses standardized questions with an
established set of answers.
   a. nondirective
   b. structured
   c. situational
   d. behavioral description

LO 3 _____ 20. Panel interviews involve
   a. one person meeting with 3 to 5 interviewers.
   b. multiple inputs regarding the applicant.
   c. shorter decision-making periods.
   d. all of the above.

LO 3 _____ 21. The type of interview that is <u>not</u> a supplemental type of interview is the
_____ interview.
   a. conventional
   b. computer
   c. phone
   d. none of the above

LO 4 _____ 22. Cognitive ability tests are valuable for assessing all of the following
except
   a. verbal.
   b. quantitative.
   c. physical.
   d. reasoning.

LO 4 _____ 23. The _____ test is best used for career development.
   a. cognitive
   b. job knowledge
   c. personality and interest
   d. physical ability

LO 4 _____ 24. One of the drawbacks of using preemployment testing is
   a. the potential for legal challenges.
   b. they are all highly subjective.
   c. they lack any validity or reliability.
   d. their use has been limited to only a few organizations.

LO 4 _____ 25. HR tests have been used most commonly
   a. in government.
   b. in big business.
   c. in small business.
   d. none of the above.

LO 4 _____ 26. Job knowledge tests include
    a. the Uniform CPA Examination.
    b. most civil service examinations.
    c. tests for those seeking to become pilots in the armed services.
    d. all of the above.

LO 4 _____ 27. An assessment center is all of the following except
    a. a process to evaluate candidates.
    b. a series of activities such as in-basket exercises and role-playing.
    c. upon completion, observations are combined to develop an overall picture of participants.
    d. a place where assessments occur.

LO 5 _____ 28. In the clinical approach to selecting an applicant,
    a. the applicant must submit to a physical exam and a drug test.
    b. personal judgment is used.
    c. the approach is frequently used in the medical community.
    d. psychological tests are used.

LO 5 _____ 29. One positive thing about for the use of the clinical approach is that
    a. those making the decision first review the data on the applicants.
    b. different individuals reach the same decision about the applicant.
    c. biases and stereotypes are revealed and then dismissed.
    d. the result is a heterogeneous workforce.

LO 5 _____ 30. Which is true about statistical approaches in the selection process?
    a. all use a compensatory approach.
    b. each requires a decision on the cutoff scores below which. an applicant is rejected.
    c. all involve a multiple cutoff to some degree.
    d. all make use of a multiple hurdle model.

True/False

Identify the following statements as True or False.

Learning Outcome (LO)

LO 1 _____ 1. The selection process should begin with the job analysis.

LO 1 _____ 2. Complete and clear job specifications differentiate between qualified and unqualified interviewers.

LO 1 _____ 3. Job specifications increase the effect of an interviewers biases and prejudices.

LO 1 _____ 4. The number of steps in the selection process and their sequence will vary.

LO 1 _____ 5. The selection process is used for existing jobs rather than projected job openings.

LO 2 _____ 6. Reliability refers to the consistency of test scores over time and across measures.

LO 2 _____ 7. Validity refers to the accuracy of the measurements taken in the selection process.

LO 2 _____ 8. Content validity refers to whether the test accurately measures what it purports to measure.

LO 2 _____ 9. Predictive validity refers to whether the test scores correlate with the job specification.

LO 2 _____ 10. Construct validity refers to whether the measurement is based on whether the test was constructed by an HR manager.

LO 2 _____ 11. Firms operating nationally have difficulty using one form due to differences in state FEPs.

LO 2 _____ 12. Depending on the state, it is a good idea for an employer to state on an application form that all employees are hired *at will*.

LO 3 _____ 13. Nonstructured interviews have been found to be better predictors of the performance of job applicants than structured interviews.

LO 3 _____ 14. It is okay but it is not necessary to train interviewers in interviewing methods.

LO 3 _____ 15. Training of interviewers should make them more aware of the job and its requirements.

LO 3 _____ 16. A sequential interview involves multiple interviews with one person over a period of time.

LO 3 _____ 17. Video interviews offer the benefit of cost.

LO 3 _____ 18. Interviewers may not ask applicants about national origin but may ask if the applicant is legally prevented from working in the United States.

LO 3 _____   19. Interviews may not ask disabled applicants regarding their ability to perform job functions.

LO 4 _____   20. Preemployment tests are more objective than interviews.

LO 4 _____   21. Preemployment tests include one that determines whether the applicant can perform the job without further training.

LO 4 _____   22. Normally, medical exams may be used prior to offering employment.

LO 5 _____   23. The statistical approach is used more commonly than the clinical approach to employment decision-making.

LO 5 _____   24. Compensatory models allow a candidates high score on one predictor to make up for a low score on another predictor.

LO 5 _____   25. The multiple hurdle involves several stages and cutoff levels.

Matching

Match each term with the proper definition.

Terms

a. behavioral description interview (BDI)
b. compensatory model
c. concurrent validity
d. construct validity
e. content validity
f. criterion-related validity
g. cross-validation
h. multiple cutoff model
i. multiple hurdle model
j. negligent hiring
k. nondirective interview

l. panel interview
m. predictive validity
n. preemployment test
o. reliability
p. selection
q. selection ratio
r. sequential interview
s. situational interview
t. structured interview
u. validity
v. validity generalization
w. virtual interviews
x. video résumés

Definitions

_____ 1.   the process of choosing individuals who have relevant qualifications to fill existing or projected job openings.

_____ 2.   an interview in which an applicant is asked about what he or she actually did in a given situation.

_____ 3.   the extent to which applicants' test scores match criterion data obtained from those applicants/employees after they have been on the job for some indefinite period.

_____ 4.   an interview in which the applicant is allowed the maximum amount of freedom in determining the course of the discussion, while the interviewer carefully refrains from influencing the applicant's remarks.

_____ 5.   an objective and standardized measure of a sample of behavior that is used to gauge a person's knowledge, skills, abilities, and other characteristics (KSAOs) relative to other individuals.

_____ 6.   the extent to which test scores (or other predictor information) match criterion data obtained at about the same time from current employees.

_____ 7.   a sequential strategy in which only applicants with the highest scores at an initial test stage go on to subsequent stages.

_____ 8.   the degree to which interviews, tests, and other selection procedures yield comparable data over time and alternative measures.

_____ 9.   a format in which a candidate is interviewed by multiple people, one right after another.

_____ 10.   the extent to which validity coefficients can be generalized across situations.

_____ 11.   the extent to which a selection instrument, such as a test, adequately samples the knowledge and skills needed to perform a particular job.

_____ 12.   an interview in which an applicant is given a hypothetical incident and asked how he or she would respond to it.

_____ 13.   degree to which a test or selection procedure measures a person's attributes.

_____ 14.   verifying the results obtained from a validation study by administering a test or test battery to a different sample (drawn from the same population).

_____ 15. an interview in which a board of interviewers questions and observes a single candidate.

_____ 16. selection decision model in which a high score in one area can make up for a low score in another area.

_____ 17. the number of applicants compared with the number of persons hired.

_____ 18. the extent to which a selection tool predicts, or significantly correlates with, important elements of work behavior.

_____ 19. selection decision model that requires an applicant to achieve some minimum level of proficiency on all selection dimensions.

_____ 20. an interview in which a set of standardized questions with an established set of answers is used.

_____ 21. the extent to which a selection tool measures a theoretical construct or trait.

_____ 22. what companies can be held liable for if they fail to make adequate background checks.

_____ 23. interviews conducted via videoconferencing or over the web.

_____ 24. videotaped résumés submitted via CD, posted online, etc.

Internet Exercises

Why are employment tests so critical?
http://www.findarticles.com/p/articles/mi_m3495/is_2_47/ai_83058935/print.
Why are situational interviews so helpful to employers?
http://www.findarticles.com/p/articles/mi_m0DTI/is_1_32/ai_n9778435/print.

How to Effectively Write a Résumé and Successfully Prepare for an Interview

1. You should understand the guidelines for an effective résumé. A résumé should include:
- *Personal identification information:* List your name, address, telephone number, email address, and so on.
- *Résumé objectives:* What are you looking for in terms of a job? Relate these objectives to your career goals.
- *Education:* This section should support and be directly correlated with your objectives. Include courses taken as well as specific skills developed through these courses, such as computer skills, problem-solving skills, and communication skills.

- *Work experience:* This information should relate to the occupational fields in which you have worked. Make sure this information indicates that you have held a job over a period of time. Highlight transferable skills related to leadership, conflict resolution, time management, and stress management activities.
- *Awards, activities, and/or military experience:* Include community experience, voluntarism (food banks, scouting programs, etc.), and/or professional memberships, such as Rotary, Kiwanis, Lions, etc.

1. To develop a competitive advantage in preparation for an interview, you should do the following:

- *Research the firm:* The library and Chamber of Commerce are excellent sources of information pertaining to a local business enterprise. Two specific sources are *The Wall Street Journal*'s "Index to Businesses" and *Standard and Poor's* "Industry Surveys."
- *Complete application forms:* Use proper English grammar and spelling. Answer all application questions at the appropriate level of detail.
- *Prepare for the interview:* Anticipate questions pertaining to your level of education, work experience, and awards and activities. Have questions for the recruiter following the interview, such as: How soon do you plan to fill this position? What growth opportunities, career development programs, orientation and training activities, and so on are available?
- *References and background investigations:* Ask for permission before using any individual's name for a reference.

SOLUTIONS

Multiple Choice:	True/False:	Matching:
1. d	1. True	1. p
2. c	2. False	2. a
3. a	3. False	3. m
4. b	4. True	4. k
5. c	5. False	5. n
6. b	6. True	6. c
7. a	7. True	7. i
8. c	8. False	8. o
9. c	9. False	9. r
10. a	10. False	10. v
11. c	11. True	11. e
12. b	12. True	12. s
13. c	13. False	13. u
14. c	14. False	14. g
15. a	15. True	15. l
16. a	16. False	16. b

17.	d	17.	True	17.	q
18.	c	18.	True	18.	f
19.	b	19.	False	19.	h
20.	d	20.	True	20.	t
21.	a	21.	True	21.	d
22.	c	22.	False	22.	j
23.	c	23.	False	23.	w
24.	a	24.	True	24.	x
25.	a	25.	True		
26.	d				
27.	d				
28.	b				
29.	a				
30.	b				

False Statements Made True

2. Complete and clear job specifications differentiate between qualified and unqualified **applicants.**

3. Job specifications **reduce** the effect of an interviewers biases and prejudices.

5. The selection process is used for **both** existing jobs **and** projected job openings.

8. Content validity refers to whether the test **was based on the job specification.**

9. Predictive validity refers to **whether the test scores correlate with performance criteria.**

10. Construct validity refers to whether it measures what it purports to measure.

13. **Structured** interviews have been found to be better predictors of the performance of job applicants than **nonstructured** interviews.

14. **It is** necessary to train interviewers in interviewing methods.

16. A sequential interview involves multiple **people** with one person **one right after another.**

19. Interviewers **may** ask disabled applicants regarding their ability to perform job functions.

22. Normally, medical exams may **not** be used prior to offering employment.

23. The **clinical** approach is used more commonly than the **statistical** approach to employment decision-making.

CHAPTER 7

TRAINING AND DEVELOPMENT

In this chapter, you will learn the systems approach to training and development and be able to describe the components of training-needs assessment. You will be able to identify the principles of learning and explain how they facilitate training. In this chapter, you will learn the types of training methods used for managers and nonmanagers. You will be able to discuss the advantages and disadvantages of various evaluation criteria. Finally, you will learn about the special training programs that are currently popular.

LEARNING OUTCOMES

After studying this chapter, you should be able to

LEARNING OUTCOME 1   Discuss the strategic approach to training and development.

LEARNING OUTCOME 2   Describe the components of a training needs assessment.

LEARNING OUTCOME 3   Identify the principles of learning and describe how they facilitate training.

LEARNING OUTCOME 4   Identify the types of training methods used for managers and non-managers.

LEARNING OUTCOME 5   Discuss the advantages and disadvantages of various evaluation criteria.

LEARNING OUTCOME 6   Describe additional training programs often conducted by firms.

CHAPTER SUMMARY RELATING TO LEARNING OUTCOMES

`LEARNING OUTCOME` The types of training given employees range from simple, on-the-job instruction to sophisticated skills training conducted on multimillion dollar simulators. Training programs cover a broad range of subjects and involve personnel at all levels. The goal of training is to contribute to an organization's overall strategic goals. To be effective, training programs need to be developed systematically. This approach consists of four phases: (1) needs assessment, (2) program design, (3) implementation, and (4) evaluation.

`LEARNING OUTCOME 2` The needs assessment phase begins with an organization analysis. Managers must establish a context for training by deciding where training is needed, how it connects with their firms' strategic goals, and how their companies' resources can best be used in terms of training. A task analysis is used to identify the knowledge, skills, and abilities employees need. A person analysis is used to identify which people need training.

`LEARNING OUTCOME 3` When designing a training program, managers must consider the two fundamental preconditions for learning: readiness and motivation of trainees. In addition, the principles of learning should be considered to create an environment that is conducive to learning. These principles include goal setting, the meaningfulness of presentation, modeling, individual differences, active practice and repetition, whole-versus-part learning, massed-versus-distributed learning, and feedback and reinforcement.

`LEARNING OUTCOME` A wide variety of methods are available to train nonmanagerial personnel. On-the-job training is one of the most commonly used methods because it provides trainees with hands-on experience and an opportunity to build a relationship with their supervisor and coworkers. Apprenticeship training and internships are especially effective. Classroom training is still the most popular way to train employees. However, programmed instruction, computer-based training, simulations, and interactive e-learning utilizing teleconferencing, video conferencing, webinars, the communities of practice method, and other means are becoming more popular. Using multiple methods or what is called blended learning, has been found to be most effective.

The training and development of managers is becoming increasingly critical for firms because they are facing increasing competition from across the globe and the baby boomer generation in the United States is retiring. A wide variety of training methods are used for developing managers. On-the-job experiences include coaching, understudy assignment, job rotation, lateral transfers, project and committee assignments, and staff meetings. Off-the-job experiences include analysis of case studies, management games and simulations, role-playing, and behavior modeling. Tuition assistance programs and corporate universities are other tools organizations utilize to help train employees for leadership positions.

`LEARNING OUTCOME` The evaluation of a training program should focus on several criteria: participants' reactions, the amount of learning they have acquired, their behavioral changes on the job, and bottom-line results such as the program's return on investment. The transfer of training is measured via examination of the degree to which trained skills are demonstrated back on the job. Benchmarking and utility analysis help evaluate the impact of training and provide the information for further needs assessment.

LEARNING OUTCOME 6   In addition to training that addresses the KSAs of a particular job, many employers develop additional training programs for various purposes. Orientation training allows new hires to more quickly acquire the knowledge, skills, and attitudes that increase the probabilities of their success within the organization. Onboarding programs go beyond orientation by bringing new hires into an organization's fold so that they truly feel like they are a part of it. This is important because new hires are at a high risk of quitting. Basic skills training, team and cross-training, ethics training, and diversity training are other programs commonly conducted by organizations.

REVIEW QUESTIONS

Multiple Choice

Choose the letter of the word or phrase that best completes each statement.

Learning Outcome (LO)

LO 1 _____   1. From the broadest perspective, the goal of training is to
   a. impart skills and knowledge.
   b. contribute to the organization's overall goals.
   c. help people to become more productive.
   d. help individuals be the best that they can be.

LO 1 _____   2. When what the competition is doing becomes the basis for a firm's training agenda, the result may be
   a. training programs that are misdirected.
   b. an ability to gain insight into the competition.
   c. an opportunity to take both the competitors' employees and customers.
   d. none of the above.

LO 2 _____   3. The top company executive responsible for making certain that training is timely and focused on the firm's top strategic issues is
   a. chief learning officer.
   b. chief executive officer.
   c. chief ethics officer.
   d. chief training officer.

LO 2 _____   4. The examination of the environment, strategies, and resources of the organization to determine where training emphasis should be placed is
   a. management by objectives.
   b. critical incident.
   c. organization analysis.
   d. job ranking.

LO 2 _____   5. Reviewing the job description and specifications to identify the activities needed to perform a particular job and the knowledge, skills, and aptitudes needed to perform those activities involves
   a. personality enhancement.
   b. the socialization process.
   c. behavior modification.
   d. task analysis.

LO 2 _____   6. This focuses on the set of skills and knowledge employees need to be successful, particularly for decision-oriented and knowledge-intensive jobs.
   a. personality assessment.
   b. the socialization assessment.
   c. behavior assessment.
   d. competency assessment.

LO 2 _____   7. The process of determining which individual employees need training and which individuals do not is
   a. person analysis.
   b. job evaluation.
   c. job analysis.
   d. employee orientation.

LO 2 _____   8. The success of a firm's training program is dependent upon
   a. employee orientation.
   b. performance appraisal.
   c. job analysis.
   d. training design.

LO 2 _____   9. As a result of conducting organization task and person analyses, managers will have a more complete picture of the training needs when they can state the desired outcomes of training through written
   a. employee contracts.
   b. job specifications.
   c. instructional objectives.
   d. implied contracts.

LO 2 _____   10. Two preconditions for learning affecting the success of those who are to receive training are
   a. readiness and motivation.
   b. task identity and task significance.
   c. behavior and personality.
   d. culture and the socialization process.

LO 3 _____ 11. Training programs are likely to be more effective if they incorporate the
   a. principles of learning.
   b. orientation program.
   c. selection process.
   d. assessment program.

LO 3 _____ 12. As an employee's training progresses, feedback serves two related purposes, which are
   a. employee probation and career development.
   b. knowledge of results and employee motivation.
   c. job security and job protection.
   d. employee results and performance evaluation.

LO 4 _____ 13. Training that provides both hands-on experience under normal working conditions and opportunities for the trainer, manager, or senior employee to build good relationships with new employees is called
   a. cooperative training.
   b. on-the-job training.
   c. competency assessment.
   d. behavior modification.

LO 4 _____ 14. The most common training method used to train nonmanagerial employees is
   a. simulation training.
   b. on-the-job training.
   c. e-learning.
   d. behavior modification.

LO 4 _____ 15. Training programs that require cooperation between organizations and their labor unions, between industry and government, or between organizations and local school systems are
   a. work seminars.
   b. career development programs.
   c. job rotation activities.
   d. apprenticeship programs.

LO 4 _____ 16. The type of training that combines practical on-the-job experience with formal classes is known as
   a. on-the-job training.
   b. vestibule training.
   c. job instruction training.
   d. cooperative training.

LO 4 _____ 17. A program that is jointly sponsored by colleges, universities, and a variety of organizations and that offers students the chance to get real-world experience while finding out how they will perform in work settings is a(n)
a. coaching technique.
b. mentor.
c. performance evaluation.
d. internship program.

LO 4 _____ 18. Training that is particularly effective in allowing individual trainees to work at their own pace is called
a. on-the-job training.
b. programmed instruction.
c. apprenticeship training.
d. cooperative training.

LO 4 _____ 19. The audiovisual, programmed, and computer-oriented training methods are evolving into what trainers today refer to as
a. e-learning.
b. on-the-job training.
c. job instruction.
d. vestibule training.

LO 4 _____ 20. A training method that emphasizes realism in equipment and its operation at minimum cost and maximum safety is known as a(n)
a. internship program.
b. on-the-job training program.
c. work sampling method.
d. simulation method.

LO 4 _____ 21. Assuming the attitudes and behavior of others involved in a particular problem is known as
a. job instruction training.
b. role playing.
c. orientation.
d. anxiety training.

LO 4 _____ 22. What term is used to describe training methods that use multiple techniques?
a. job instruction training.
b. role playing.
c. orientation.
d. blended learning.

LO 5 _____ 23. The following basic criteria are available to evaluate training programs, *except*
   a. learning.
   b. predictions.
   c. behavior.
   d. results.

LO 5 _____ 24. One of the simplest and most common approaches to training evaluation is assessing
   a. employee needs.
   b. leadership styles.
   c. coaching techniques.
   d. participant reactions.

LO 6 _____ 25. Managers must clearly define the measures of competency and performance and must objectively assess the current situation and identify areas for improvement when using
   a. quality circles.
   b. vestibule training.
   c. benchmarking.
   d. on-the-job training.

LO 6 _____ 26. The formal process of familiarizing new employees with the organization, their jobs, and their work unit is
   a. team training.
   b. diversity training.
   c. sensitivity training.
   d. orientation training.

LO 6 _____ 27. Learning essential occupational qualifications having profound implications for product quality, customer service, internal efficiency, and workplace and environmental safety is known as
   a. job instruction training.
   b. basic skills training.
   c. on-the-job training.
   d. coaching and mentoring.

LO 6 _____ 28. High-ranking managers responsible for fostering the ethical climate within their firms are called
   a. chief learning officer.
   b. chief executive officer.
   c. chief ethics officer.
   d. chief training officer.

LO 6 _____   29. An awareness of the varied demographics of the workforce, the
                     challenges of affirmative action, the dynamics of stereotyping, the
                     changing values of the workforce, and the potential competitive payoffs
                     from bringing different people together for a common purpose is known
                     as
                     a. diversity training.
                     b. basic skills training.
                     c. on-the-job training.
                     d. computer-assisted training.

LO 6 _____   30. To avoid the pitfalls of substandard diversity training, managers will
                     want to do the following, *except*
                     a. forge a strategic link.
                     b. check out consultant qualifications.
                     c. analyze and review performance appraisal methods.
                     d. choose training methods carefully.

True/False

Identify the following statements as True or False.

Learning Outcome (LO)

LO 1 _____   1. From the broadest perspective, the goal of training is to contribute to an
                    organization's survival.

LO 1 _____   2. Training programs that are widely adopted by other firms should be a
                    strategic imperative for one's own firm.

LO 1 _____   3. To have maximum impact, a firm should have a four-phase approach in
                    which the first phase involves program design.

LO 2 _____   4. Task analysis involves reviewing the job description and specifications
                    to identify the activities performed in a particular job and the knowledge,
                    skills, and aptitudes (KSAs) needed to perform them.

LO 2 _____   5. Person analysis involves determining which employees require training
                    and, equally important, which do not.

LO 2 _____   6. Most employees are motivated by certain common needs and are similar
                    in the relative importance of these needs at any given time.

LO 3 _____   7. The value of goal setting for focusing and motivating behavior extends
                    into training.

LO 3 _____ 8. Even modeling the wrong behavior can be helpful if it shows trainees what not to do and if the appropriate behavior is then demonstrated.

LO 3 _____ 9. Feedback is simply the feeling of accomplishment that follows successful performance of training.

LO 3 _____ 10. The success of any training effort will depend in large part on the teaching skills and personal characteristics of those responsible for conducting the training.

LO 4 _____ 11. All types of organizations use on-the-job training (OJT), and it is one of the most efficiently implemented training methods.

LO 4 _____ 12. With apprenticeship training, thorough instruction and experience, both on and off the job, in the practical and theoretical aspects of the work are given to individuals entering the industry.

LO 4 _____ 13. The term "cooperative training" is typically used in connection with high school and college programs that incorporate part-time or full-time job experiences.

LO 4 _____ 14. The programmed training method lends itself particularly to training in areas where information can be presented in lectures, demonstrations, films, and videotapes or through computer instruction.

LO 4 _____ 15. While programmed instruction increases the amount an individual learns, it typically decreases the speed at which he or she learns.

LO 4 _____ 16. By presenting managers with the opportunities to perform under pressure and to learn from their mistakes, on-the-job development experiences are some of the most powerful and commonly used techniques.

LO 4 _____ 17. Seminars and conferences, unlike classroom instruction, are useful for bringing groups of people together for training and development.

LO 5 _____ 18. Testing knowledge and skills before beginning a training program gives a baseline standard on trainees that can be measured again after training to determine improvement.

LO 5 _____ 19. Basic-skills training is the formal process of familiarizing new employees with the organization, their jobs, and their work units.

LO 5 _____ 20. To evaluate benchmarking standards, the late W. Edwards Deming's classic four-step process for needs assessment advocates that managers plan, do, check, and act.

LO 5 _____   21. To use benchmarking successfully in training, managers must clearly define the measures of competency and performance and must objectively assess the current situation and identify areas of improvement.

LO 6 _____   22. To get new employees off to a good start, organizations generally offer a formal orientation program.

LO 6 _____   23. The supervisor has the least important role in the orientation program.

LO 6 _____   24. While there are different possible approaches to ensuring that employees have basic skills, the establishment of in-house basic skills programs has decreased in favor.

LO 6 _____   25. Organizations that have been successful with diversity training realize that it is a long-term process that requires the highest level of skill.

Matching

Match each term with the proper definition.

Terms

a.	apprenticeship training	l.	instructional objectives
b.	behavior modeling	m.	just-in time training
c.	behavior modification	n.	learning management system
d.	benchmarking	o.	on-the-job training (OJT)
e.	blended learning	p.	onboarding
f.	chief ethics officer	q.	organization analysis
g.	chief learning officer	r.	orientation
h.	competency assessment	s.	person analysis
i.	cooperative training	t.	spot rewards
j.	cross-training	u.	task analysis
k.	e-learning	v.	transfer of training

Definitions

_____   1. an examination of the environment, strategies, and resources of the organization to determine where training emphasis should be placed.

_____   2. process of systematically socializing new employees to help them get "on board" with an organization.

_____ 3. formal process of familiarizing new employees with the organization, their jobs, and their work units.

_____ 4. training program that combines practical on-the-job experience with formal educational classes.

_____ 5. effective application of principles to what is required on the job.

_____ 6. system of training in which a worker entering the skilled trades is given thorough instruction and experience, both on and off the job, in the practical and theoretical aspects of the work.

_____ 7. determines which employees require training and which do not.

_____ 8. process of determining what the content of a training program should be on the basis of a study of the tasks or duties involved in the job.

_____ 9. desired outcomes of a training program.

_____ 10. approach that demonstrates desired behavior and gives trainees the chance to practice and role-play those behaviors and receive feedback.

_____ 11. method by which employees are given hands-on experience with instructions from their supervisor or other trainer.

_____ 12. process of measuring an organization's own services and practices against the recognized industry leaders in order to identify areas for improvement.

_____ 13. analysis of the sets of skills and knowledge needed for decision-oriented and knowledge-intensive jobs.

_____ 14. technique that operates on the principle that behavior that is rewarded or positively reinforced will be exhibited more frequently in the future, whereas behavior that is penalized or unrewarded will decrease in frequency.

_____ 15. the process of training employees to do multiple jobs within the organization.

_____ 16. audiovisual, programmed, and computer-oriented training methods.

_____ 17. training methods that use multiple techniques.

_____ 18. high ranking manager responsible for fostering the ethical climate within the firm.

_____ 19. top company executive responsible for making certain that training is timely and focused on the firm's top strategic issues.

_____ 20. providing training opportunities to employees where and when they need them.

_____ 21. combination of e-learning, employee assessment tools, and other training functions.

_____ 22. programs that award employees "on the spot" when they do something particularly well during training or on the job.

Internet Exercises

How can companies tell whether on-the-job training has been worth it?
http://www.findarticles.com/p/articles/mi_m0DTI/is_10_31/ai_n6335227.

What is an internship and why should a student do one?
http://careerservices.class.umn.edu/students/internships.html

How to Begin Orientation and Training

1. How would you inquire about and prepare for orientation and training programs? During the interview, you should inquire about the orientation and training you will receive once hired. To minimize anxiety, an orientation program should address the job description, the people or employees you are expected to work with, and the crossover between departments. A checklist will help you focus on information relevant to performance of the job. Ask questions such as the following about the training programs offered to new employees: What are the objectives of the training program? What type of training program is used? How is the training program evaluated? How long is the training program? How often are individuals retrained? Is retraining continuous?

2. As a student, how important is it to know how to benefit from an organization's orientation and training program? A new recruit should work with the Human Resources Department and learn everything about the organization's policies, procedures, and rules. Ask for an occupational manual to learn everything you can about the new job.

SOLUTIONS

Multiple Choice:		True/False:		Matching:	
1.	b	1.	False	1.	q
2.	a	2.	False	2.	p
3.	a	3.	False	3.	r
4.	c	4.	True	4.	i
5.	d	5.	True	5.	v
6.	d	6.	False	6.	a
7.	a	7.	True	7.	s
8.	d	8.	True	8.	u
9.	c	9.	False	9.	l
10.	a	10.	True	10.	b
11.	a	11.	False	11.	o
12.	b	12.	True	12.	d
13.	b	13.	True	13.	h
14.	b	14.	False	14.	c
15.	d	15.	False	15.	j
16.	d	16.	True	16.	k
17.	d	17.	False	17.	e
18.	b	18.	True	18.	f
19.	a	19.	False	19.	g
20.	d	20.	True	20.	m
21.	b	21.	True	21.	n
22.	d	22.	True	22.	t
23.	b	23.	False		
24.	d	24.	False		
25.	c	25.	True		
26.	d				
27.	b				
28.	c				
29.	a				
30.	c				

False Statements Made True

1. From the broadest perspective, the goal of training is to contribute to an organization's **overall goals.**

2. Training programs that are widely adopted by other firms should **not** be a strategic imperative for one's own firm.

3. To have maximum impact, a firm should have a four phase approach in which the first phase involves **needs assessment**.

6. **While** most employees are motivated by certain common needs, they **differ from one another** in the relative importance of these needs at any given time.

9. **Reinforcement** is simply the feeling of accomplishment that follows successful performance of training.

11. All types of organizations use on-the-job training (OJT); **however,** it is one of the most **poorly** implemented training methods.

14. The **classroom** training method lends itself particularly to training in areas where information can be presented in lectures, demonstrations, films, and videotapes or through computer instruction.

15. While programmed instruction **may not increase** the amount an individual learns, it typically **increases** the speed at which he or she learns.

17. Seminars and conferences, **like** classroom instruction, are useful for bringing groups of people together for training and development.

19. **Orientation** is the formal process of familiarizing new employees with the organization, their jobs, and their work units.

23. The supervisor has the **most** important role in the orientation program.

24. While there are different possible approaches to ensuring that employees have basic skills, the establishment of in-house basic skills programs has **come increasingly into** favor.

CHAPTER 8

PERFORMANCE MANAGEMENT AND THE EMPLOYEE APPRAISAL PROCESS

A major function of human resources management is the appraisal and improvement of employee performance. In establishing a performance appraisal program, managers should give careful attention to its objectives and to the criteria against which employees are to be evaluated. Court decisions have emphasized the importance of having carefully defined and measurable criteria. Newer methods and techniques for appraisal are replacing some of the older methods that are more subject to errors. The methods used should be consistent with the objectives of appraisal in the particular organization. Through interviews, managers can give information from the appraisal to subordinates and make plans for improving performance.

LEARNING OUTCOMES

After studying this chapter, you should be able to

LEARNING OUTCOME 1 Explain what performance management is and how the establishment of goals, ongoing performance feedback, and the appraisal process are part of it.

LEARNING OUTCOME 2 Explain the purposes of performance appraisals and the reasons they sometimes fail.

LEARNING OUTCOME 3 Describe the different sources of appraisal information.

LEARNING OUTCOME 4 Explain the various methods used to evaluate the performance of employees.

LEARNING OUTCOME 5 Outline the characteristics of an effective performance appraisal interview.

CHAPTER SUMMARY RELATING TO LEARNING OUTCOMES

LEARNING OUTCOME   Performance management is the process of creating a work environment in which people can perform to the best of their abilities to meet a company's goals. Performance appraisals are the result of an annual, biannual, or quarterly process in which a manager evaluates an employee's performance relative to the requirements of his or her job and uses the information to show the person where improvements are needed and why. Appraisals are just part of the performance management process, however. Aligning the goals of employees with that of the firm, providing employees with continual on-the-job feedback, and rewarding them are critical as well.

LEARNING OUTCOME 2   Performance appraisal programs serve many purposes, but in general, those purposes can be clustered into two categories: administrative and developmental. The administrative purposes include decisions about who will be promoted, transferred, or laid off. Appraisals are also conducted to make compensation decisions. Developmental decisions include those related to improving and enhancing an individual's capabilities. These include identifying a person's strengths and weaknesses, eliminating external performance obstacles, and establishing training needs.

Some human resource experts and firms believe performance appraisals are ineffective. In other organizations, performance appraisals are seen as a necessary evil. Managers frequently avoid conducting appraisals because they dislike passing judgment on people. Furthermore, if managers are not adequately trained, subjectivity and organizational politics can distort employee reviews. The do not develop good feedback skills and are often not prepared to conduct an appraisal. As a consequence, the appraisal is done begrudgingly once a year and then forgotten. The ultimate success or failure of a performance appraisal program depends on the philosophy underlying it, its connection with the firm's business goals, and the attitudes and skills of those responsible for its administration.

LEARNING OUTCOME 3   Appraisal information can be derived from a variety of sources, including an employee's supervisor, peers, customers, suppliers, subordinates as well as the employee being appraised. However, the raters need training so the appraisals are reliable, strategically relevant, and free from either criterion deficiency or criterion contamination. Appraisal systems must also comply with the law and, like selections tests, be valid and reliable. For example, ratings must be job-related, employees must understand their performance standards in advance, appraisers must be able to observe job performance, appraisers must be trained, feedback must be given, and an appeals procedure must be established. Some companies now hold calibration meetings to ensure their managers are accurately rating employees. Using multiple raters is frequently a good idea because different individuals see different facets of an employee's performance. An increasing number of organizations are using 360-degree appraisals to get a more comprehensive picture of how well their employees are performing. Regardless of the source of appraisal information, appraisers should be thoroughly trained in the particular methods they will use in evaluating their subordinates.

`LEARNING OUTCOME`   Several methods can be used for performance appraisals. These include trait approaches (such as graphic rating scales, mixed standard scales, forced-choice forms, and essays), behavioral methods (such as critical incident ratings, checklists, BARS, and BOS), and results methods (MBO). The choice of method depends on the purpose of the appraisal. Trait appraisals are simple to develop and complete, but they have problems in terms of their subjectivity and are not useful for feedback. Behavioral methods provide more specific information for giving feedback but can be time-consuming and costly to develop. Results appraisals are more objective and can link individual performance to the organization as a whole, but they may encourage a short-term perspective (such as annual goals) and may not include subtle yet important aspects of performance.

`LEARNING OUTCOME 5`   The degree to which a performance appraisal program benefits an organization and its members is directly related to the quality of the appraisal interviews that are conducted. Interviewing skills are best developed through instruction and supervised practice. Although there are various approaches to the interview, research suggests that employee participation and goal setting lead to higher satisfaction and improved performance. Discussing problems with employees, showing support for them, minimizing criticism, and rewarding them when they perform well are also beneficial practices. During the interview, performance deficiencies can be discussed and plans for improvement can be made.

REVIEW QUESTIONS

Multiple Choice

Choose the letter of the word or phrase that best completes each statement.

Learning Outcome (LO)

LO 1 _____   1. _____ is part of _____.
     a. performance management, performance appraisal
     b. performance appraisal, performance management
     c. performance management, nothing else
     d. performance appraisal, nothing else

LO 1 _____   2. Performance feedback to a sales person should be given
     a. at the annual performance appraisal.
     b. once a month.
     c. once a week.
     d. b and/or c above.

LO 2 _____   3. The text uses the saying "what gets measured gets done" in reference to
   a. performance appraisal.
   b. quantitative methods.
   c. measurement of production.
   d. college tests.

LO 2 _____   4. Which is not a developmental reason for performance appraisal?
   a. provide performance feedback.
   b. identify individual strengths and weaknesses.
   c. document personnel decisions.
   d. recognize individual achievements.

LO 2 _____   5. The four basic elements to be considered when establishing performance standards do **not** include
   a. strategic relevance.
   b. criterion deficiency.
   c. criterion contamination.
   d. the individual employee.

LO 2 _____   6. _____ can be measured by correlating two sets of ratings by a single rater or two different raters.
   a. strategic relevance
   b. criterion deficiency
   c. criterion contamination
   d. reliability

LO 2 _____   7. _____ is the extent to which the standards capture the entire range of an employee's responsibilities.
   a. strategic relevance
   b. criterion deficiency
   c. criterion contamination
   d. reliability

LO 2 _____   8. _____ pertains to factors outside an employee's control that affect his or her performance.
   a. strategic relevance
   b. criterion deficiency
   c. criterion contamination
   d. reliability

LO 2 _____   9. _____ is a process intended to ensure that various employee appraisals are in line with each other.
    a. calibration
    b. contamination
    c. criterion
    d. analysis

LO 2 _____   10. A rating error caused by comparing an employee to another person who was just previously rated.
    a. comparison.
    b. conviction.
    c. contrast.
    d. causal.

LO 3 _____   11. Which is not true of a self-appraisal?
    a. it is generally completed on an appraisal form.
    b. it is also known as a subordinate appraisal.
    c. it is completed by the employee.
    d. it is completed prior to the performance interview.

LO 3 _____   12. Which is true of self-appraisal?
    a. it can be a valuable source of information.
    b. critics argue that self-raters are less lenient on themselves than managers.
    c. there is no evidence that self-raters believe they can influence the outcome of the appraisal.
    d. the self-appraisal is not useful for developmental purposes.

LO 3 _____   13. Compared to performance appraisals by supervisors, peer appraisals
    a. may furnish more accurate and valid information.
    b. are based on more frequent and realistic observations.
    c. could be a popularity contest.
    d. all of the above.

LO 3 _____   14. A team appraisal
    a. is an appraisal of the team as a group rather than individuals by a manager.
    b. is a self-appraisal of the team by its members.
    c. is an extension of the peer appraisal.
    d. is an appraisal of a manager by a team.

LO 3 _____   15. The 360-degree system
    a. is a multi rater system.
    b. is solely developmental rather than an actual appraisal.
    c. is not effective for management.
    d. lacks accuracy.

LO 3 _____   16. Intel observed the following regarding its 360-degree system
    a. each person should know the source of ratings.
    b. supervisors should interact with raters regarding their rating.
    c. raters should check for prejudices.
    d. all of the above.

LO 3 _____   17. When a rater is evaluating an employee's performance based on several rating factors but performance in one factor affects the evaluation in other unrelated factors, that is known as a _____ error.
    a. horn
    b. halo
    c. administrative
    d. a and b above

LO 4 _____   18. Measuring traits such dependability, initiative and creativity is the purpose of
    a. graphic rating scales.
    b. mixed-standard scales.
    c. forced-choice method.
    d. all of the above.

LO 4 _____   19. The essay method
    a. requires the employee to describe his or her achievements.
    b. requires the appraiser to compose a statement to rate the employee.
    c. is the fastest way to cover all aspects of the employee's performance and characteristics.
    d. tends to be the most objective form of appraisal.

LO 4 _____   20. The critical incident method
    a. uses a behavioral checklist.
    b. is an unusual event involving superior or inferior performance.
    c. involves the use of critical thinking in analyzing performance.
    d. involves criticisms of the employee's performance.

LO 4 _____ 21. _____ is the behavioral approach to performance appraisal that measures the frequency of observed behavior.
a. behaviorally anchored rating scale
b. behavioral checklist method
c. behavior observation scale
d. results method

LO 4 _____ 22. Which is true of the results method?
a. uses include evaluating sales people on sales volume, production workers on output, and the CEO on profits.
b. may produce a short-term outlook and overlook concern for human relations.
c. both results and the methods used should be considered.
d. all of the above.

LO 5 _____ 23. Which is not one of the categories used in the Balanced Scorecard?
a. employee relations.
b. financial.
c. customer.
d. processes.

LO 5 _____ 24. The _____ interview gives both managers and employees the opportunity to deal with their frustrations.
a. tell-and sell
b. tell-and listen
c. problem solving
d. impromptu

LO 5 _____ 25. In giving criticism to an employee during a performance review, one should
a. be frank and lay it on the line.
b. use a standard approach for all so as to be impartial.
c. give criticism in small doses.
d. avoid being too specific.

LO 5 _____ 26. Motivational factors that affect an employee's performance do **not** include
a. job design.
b. relations with coworkers.
c. fairness perceptions.
d. goals and expectations.

LO 5 _____   27. Which is not an activity that is part of the performance diagnosis?
      a. beginning by dealing with lack of ability.
      b. considering skill issues.
      c. examining motivational issues.
      d. evaluating the work environment.

LO 5 _____   28. Performance interviewing skills are best developed through
      a. supervision.
      b. practice.
      c. both of the above.
      d. none of the above.

LO 5 _____   29. In dealing with an ineffective employee, all of the following are
alternatives except
      a. transfer to another job or department.
      b. training to improve effectiveness.
      c. removing employee feelings as a consideration.
      d. look for new ways to motivate.

LO 5 _____   30. The manager who initially assumes that an employee does not "measure
up"
      a. usually motivates the employee to prove the manager wrong.
      b. often is engaging in a self-fulfilling prophecy.
      c. is wise to be skeptical.
      d. shows employees that the manager is not easily fooled.

True/False

Identify the following statements as True or False.

Learning Outcome (LO)

LO 1 _____   1. Performance management deals with performance, not the work
environment.

LO 1 _____   2. Performance appraisal could be compared to taking a test in college.

LO 1 _____   3. Performance feedback is most useful when it is immediate and specific
to a situation.

LO 1 _____   4. Specific examples create confusion during a feedback session.

LO 2 _____ 5. Some believe that individual performance appraisals discourage teamwork.

LO 2 _____ 6. One of the main concerns employees have about performance appraisals is fairness.

LO 2 _____ 7. In Brito v. Zia, the Supreme Court ruled that performance appraisals are **not** subject to the same validity criteria as selection procedures.

LO 2 _____ 8. In scheduling performance appraisals, do not schedule more than 10 minutes to two hours in advance so that the employee will not have time to develop excuses or complaints.

LO 2 _____ 9. When performance falls short of expectations, fire the person and use the firing as a warning to others.

LO 3 _____ 10. A subordinate appraisal is an appraisal of a superior by a subordinate.

LO 3 _____ 11. Peer appraisals are done by fellow employees and combined into a single profile.

LO 3 _____ 12. The team appraisal is based on TQM concepts.

LO 3 _____ 13. It is normally quite easy to separate out the individual's contribution to team performance.

LO 3 _____ 14. A customer appraisal is based on TQM concepts.

LO 3 _____ 15. A 360-degree system fails to provide employees with inputs from all angles.

LO 3 _____ 16. In a 360-degree system, it is important to check for prejudices and preferences regarding various groups.

LO 3 _____ 17. In a survey of 55 HR managers from medium and large companies, over half said their companies did little or no evaluation of how their managers do appraisals.

LO 4 _____ 18. Graphic rating scales consist of curves showing the rise and fall of an employees' quantity of output such as sales or units over time.

LO 4 _____ 19. Mixed standard scales are identical to the basic rating scale method.

LO 4 _____ 20. The forced-choice method requires raters to choose from statements that distinguish between successful and unsuccessful performance.

LO 4 _____ 21. MBO has employees establish objectives by consulting with their supervisors and then supervisors use those objectives to evaluate the employees.

LO 5 _____ 22. The appraisal interview is perhaps the least important part of the entire performance process.

LO 5 _____ 23. When employees are able to have inputs to the appraisal process, they are likely to be less satisfied and will demand procedural justice.

LO 5 _____ 24. When raters begin an appraisal session with praise, many employees assume that criticism will be next.

LO 5 _____ 25. When dealing with a problem area, remember that is not necessarily the person who is bad but rather the person's actions on the job.

Matching

Match each term with the proper definition.

Terms

a. behavior observation scale (BOS)
b. behaviorally anchored rating scale (BARS)
c. calibration
d. contrast error
e. critical incident
f. customer appraisal
g. error of central tendency
h. essay method
i. focal performance appraisal
j. forced-choice method
k. forced distribution
l. graphic rating-scale method
m. leniency or strictness error
n. management by objectives (MBO)
o. manager and/or supervisor appraisal
p. mixed-standard scale method
q. peer appraisal
r. performance appraisal
s. performance management
t. recency error
u. self-appraisal
v. similar-to-me error
w. subordinate appraisal
x. team appraisal

Definitions

_____ 1. a process typically delivered annually by a supervisor to a subordinate, designed to help employees understand their roles, objectives, expectations, and performance success.

_____ 2. philosophy of management that rates performance on the basis of employee achievement of goals set by the mutual agreement of employee and manager.

_____ 3. performance appraisal, based on TQM concepts, that recognizes team accomplishment rather than individual performance.

_____ 4. a behavioral approach to performance appraisal that measures the frequency of observed behavior.

_____ 5. a trait approach to performance appraisal that requires the rater to compose a statement describing employee behavior.

_____ 6. performance appraisal that, like team appraisal, is based on TQM concepts and seeks evaluation from both external and internal customers.

_____ 7. performance-rating error in which an employee's evaluation is biased either upward or downward because of comparison with another employee just previously evaluated.

_____ 8. performance-rating error in which an appraiser inflates the evaluation of an employee because of a mutual personal connection.

_____ 9. a trait approach to performance appraisal whereby each employee is rated according to a scale of characteristics.

_____ 10. performance appraisal done by one's fellow employees that are generally compiled into a single profile to be used in the performance interview conducted by the employee's manager.

_____ 11. unusual event that denotes superior or inferior employee performance in some part of the job.

_____ 12. performance appraisal of a superior by an employee, which is more appropriate for developmental than for administrative purposes.

_____ 13. performance-rating error in which all employees are rated about average.

_____ 14. a trait approach to performance appraisal similar to other scale methods but based on comparison with (better than, equal to, or worse than) a standard.

_____ 15.   a behavioral approach to performance appraisal that consists of a series of vertical scales, one for each important dimension of job performance.

_____ 16.   performance appraisal done by the employee being evaluated, generally on an appraisal form completed by the employee prior to the performance interview.

_____ 17.   performance appraisal done by an employee's manager and often reviewed by a manager one level higher.

_____ 18.   a trait approach to performance appraisal that requires the rater to choose from statements designed to distinguish between successful and unsuccessful performance.

_____ 19.   performance-rating error in which the appraiser tends to give employees either unusually high or unusually low ratings.

_____ 20.   the process of creating a work environment in which people can perform to the best of their abilities.

_____ 21.   performance-rating error in which the appraisal is based largely on the employee's most recent behavior rather than on behavior throughout the appraisal period.

_____ 22.   a process whereby managers meet to discuss the performance of individual employees to ensure their employee appraisal are in line with one another.

_____ 23.   an appraisal system in which all of an organization's employees are reviewed at the same time of year rather on the anniversaries of their individual hire dates.

_____ 24.   a performance appraisal ranking system whereby raters are required to place a certain percentage of employees into various performance categories.

Internet Exercises

What is the manager's primary responsibility toward employees?
http://www.findarticles.com/p/articles/mi_m0KJI/is_2_117/ai_n12414578.

What is the role of a team leader in managing subordinates?
http://www.findarticles.com/p/articles/mi_qa3616?is_200304/ai_n9173768.

How to Prepare for a Performance Appraisal Interview

You should understand the objective of performance appraisal. Employees need feedback to understand how secure they are within the organization. It is important that the employee knows the work activity required to perform her or his job. A performance appraisal interview will accomplish such objectives.

A performance appraisal is conducted to assess the performance of the individual in his or her job operations. There are different performance appraisal methods and different means to accomplish this activity. Traditionally, a supervisor evaluates the performance of the employee. There are also peer-based, self-directed, and customer-based methods of doing performance appraisals.

In the traditional method of interviewing, the supervisor should have a thorough understanding of the employee's job description. In addition, the performance appraisal should be put in writing and taken into the interview with the supervisor. The appraisal should be used as a basis for merit reviews and should be signed at the end of the interview to indicate that the supervisor has reviewed the performance appraisal with the employee. Finally, there should be an appeal process if the employee disagrees with the appraisal.

SOLUTIONS

Multiple Choice:	True/False:	Matching:
1. b	1. False	1. r
2. d	2. True	2. n
3. a	3. True	3. x
4. c	4. False	4. a
5. d	5. True	5. h
6. d	6. False	6. f
7. b	7. False	7. d
8. c	8. False	8. v
9. a	9. False	9. l
10. c	10. False	10. q
11. b	11. True	11. e
12. a	12. True	12. w
13. d	13. False	13. g
14. c	14. True	14. p
15. a	15. False	15. b
16. d	16. True	16. u
17. d	17. True	17. o
18. d	18. False	18. j
19. b	19. False	19. m
20. b	20. True	20. s
21. c	21. True	21. t

22. d	22. False	22. c
23. a	23. False	23. i
24. b	24. True	24. k
25. c	25. True	
26. a		
27. a		
28. c		
29. c		
30. b		

False Statements Made True

1. Performance management deals with performance, **and** the work environment.

4. **Lack of** specific examples creates confusion during a feedback session

7. In Brito v. Zia, the Supreme Court ruled that performance appraisals **are** subject to the same validity criteria as selection procedures.

8. In scheduling performance appraisals, **schedule** 10 **days** to two **weeks** in advance.

9. When performance falls short of expectations, **find out why**.

13. It is normally impossible to separate out the individual's contribution to team performance.

15. A 360-degree system **does** provide employees with inputs from all angles.

18. Graphic rating scales are **a trait approach to rating according to characteristics.**

19. Mixed standard scales are **a modification** to the basic rating scale method.

22. The appraisal interview is perhaps the **most** important part of the entire performance process.

23. When employees are able to have inputs to the appraisal process, they are likely to be **more** satisfied and will **feel they have received** procedural justice.

CHAPTER 9

MANAGING COMPENSATION

Employees seek various psychological rewards from their jobs, but this does not diminish the importance of the compensation they receive. It is essential that this compensation be equitable in terms of the job's value to the organization and in relation to the pay other employees receive. The purchasing power of workers' salaries must be adjusted upward periodically to accommodate rises in the cost of living. In addition, compensation payments must be consistent with the terms of the labor agreement, where one exists, and with state and federal regulations governing it. Issues of equal pay for comparable worth, pay compression, and low wage budgets are emerging issues in the field of management compensation.

LEARNING OUTCOMES

After studying this chapter, you should be able to

LEARNING OUTCOME 1	Explain how to formulate a strategic compensation program.
LEARNING OUTCOME 2	Indicate how pay is determined.
LEARNING OUTCOME 3	Know how to effectively perform a job evaluation.
LEARNING OUTCOME 4	Explain the purpose of a wage survey.
LEARNING OUTCOME 5	Define the wage curve, pay grades, and rate ranges as parts of the compensation structure.
LEARNING OUTCOME 6	Understand the importance of using a compensation scorecard.
LEARNING OUTCOME 7	Identify the major provisions of the federal laws affecting compensation.

114

CHAPTER SUMMARY RELATING TO LEARNING OUTCOMES

LEARNING OUTCOME   Establishing strategic compensation programs requires an assessment of organizational objectives in relation to specific employment goals—employee retention for continued growth, compensation distribution to ensure employees feel treated fairly, communication of compensation methods to increase employee understanding of organizational objectives, and adherence to a budget for cost efficiencies, for instance. Compensation must reward employees for past efforts (pay-for-performance) while motivating employees' future performance. Internal and external equity of the pay program affects employees' concepts of fairness. Organizations must balance each of these concerns while still remaining competitive. The ability to attract and retain qualified employees while controlling labor costs is a major factor in allowing organizations to remain viable in the domestic or international markets.

LEARNING OUTCOME 2   The basis on which compensation payments are determined and the way they are administered can significantly affect employee productivity and the achievement of organizational goals. Internal influences include the employer's compensation policy, worth of the job, performance of the employee, and employer's ability to pay. External factors influencing pay rates include labor market conditions, area pay rates, cost of living, outcomes of collective bargaining, and legal requirements.

LEARNING OUTCOME 3   Organizations use one of four basic job evaluation techniques to determine the relative worth of jobs. The job ranking system arranges jobs in numerical order on the basis of the importance of the job's duties and responsibilities to the organization. The job classification system slots jobs into preestablished grades. Higher-rated grades will require more responsibilities, working conditions, and job duties. The point system of job evaluation uses a point scheme based on the compensable job factors of skill, effort, responsibility, and working conditions. The more compensable factors a job possesses, the more points are assigned to it. Jobs with higher accumulated points are considered more valuable to the organization. The work valuation system evaluates jobs based on their value relative to organizational goals—financial, customer service, and so on—and the jobs' contribution to organization success.

LEARNING OUTCOME   Wage surveys determine the external equity of jobs. Data obtained from surveys will facilitate establishing the organization's wage policy while ensuring that the employer does not pay more, or less, than needed for jobs in the relevant labor market.

LEARNING OUTCOME 5   The wage structure is composed of the wage curve, pay grades, and rate ranges. The wage curve depicts graphically the pay rates assigned to jobs within each pay grade. Pay grades represent the grouping of similar jobs on the basis of their relative worth. Each pay grade will include a rate range. Rate ranges will have a midpoint and minimum and maximum pay rates for all jobs in the pay grade.

LEARNING OUTCOME 6   The effectiveness of a compensation system can be assessed by using a compensation scorecard. The scorecard collects and displays where all departments and/or functions sit in terms of their relative compensation. It increases the transparency of compensation systems, the accountability of managers, and helps companies align their compensation decisions with organizational objectives.

115

LEARNING OUTCOME 7   Both the Davis-Bacon Act and the Walsh-Healy Act are prevailing wage statutes. These laws require government contractors to pay wages normally based on the union scale in the employer's operating area. The Walsh-Healy Act also requires payment of one and one-half times the regular pay for hours over eight per day or forty per week. The Fair Labor Standards Act contains provisions covering the federal minimum wage, hours worked, and child labor. Pay rate compression is the narrowing of pay between new, less experienced employees and experienced senior employees. The primary cause of the problem is the high salaries paid to new employees and minimum wage increases. Hourly employees and their managers may experience pay compression when the salary spread between the two groups is low.

REVIEW QUESTIONS

Multiple Choice

Choose the letter of the word or phrase that best completes each statement.

Learning Outcome (LO)

LO 1 _____   1. Linking compensation to organizational objectives, the pay-for-performance standard, and the motivating value of compensation are aspects of
   a. job enlargement.
   b. strategic compensation planning.
   c. job enrichment.
   d. employee empowerment.

LO 1 _____   2. Formal statements of compensation policies typically include the following except
   a. the level of pay needed to prevent unionization.
   b. whether the rate of pay is to be above, below, or at the prevailing market rate.
   c. the level of pay at which employees may be recruited.
   d. the extent to which seniority affects pay.

LO 1 _____   3. Equity theory is also referred to as
   a. value-added theory.
   b. pay-for-performance standard.
   c. distributive fairness.
   d. competence-based theory.

LO 1 _____   4. A wide range of compensation options, including merit-based pay,
bonuses, salary commissions, job and pay banding, team/group
incentives, and various gainsharing programs, is called
a. job evaluation.
b. performance appraisal.
c. pay-for-performance.
d. management by objectives.

LO 1 _____   5. When employees believe that the wage rates for their jobs approximate
the job's worth to the organization, compensation policies are considered
to be
a. mixed combinations.
b. externally equitable.
c. paired comparisons.
d. internally equitable.

LO 1 _____   6. The situation that exists when an organization is paying wages that are
relatively equal to what other employers are paying for similar types of
work is known as
a. external pay equity.
b. comparable worth.
c. internal pay equity.
d. equity theory of motivation.

LO 1 _____   7. The theory that predicts how one's level of motivation depends on the
attractiveness of the rewards sought and the probability of obtaining
those rewards is the
a. two-factor theory of motivation.
b. equity theory of motivation.
c. expectancy theory of motivation.
d. needs hierarchy theory.

LO 1 _____   8. A system of pay in which employees are paid according to the
number of units they produce is
a. hourly work.
b. salary.
c. piecework.
d. real wages.

LO 2 _____   9. An internal factor affecting the wage mix is
a. worth of job.
b. job evaluation programs.
c. job analysis programs.
d. incentive programs.

LO 2 _____ 10. An external factor affecting the wage mix is
    a. cost of living.
    b. job evaluation programs.
    c. job analysis programs.
    d. incentive programs.

LO 2 _____ 11. In order for merit pay to be effective, a firm should do all of the following except
    a. raises should be based on steps within a rate range for a job class.
    b. an effective performance appraisal system is needed to show who deserves a merit raise.
    c. there must be a credible relationship between performance and merit raises.
    d. raises should be granted automatically.

LO 2 _____ 12. A means of wage payment that can be affected by earned profits and other financial resources available to employers is a(n)
    a. employee worth system.
    b. pay level.
    c. critical incident.
    d. job evaluation program.

LO 2 _____ 13. Due to inflation, compensation rates have been adjusted upward periodically to help employees maintain their
    a. comparable worth.
    b. job evaluation.
    c. purchasing power.
    d. noneconomic benefits.

LO 3 _____ 14. In job evaluation, jobs are classified and grouped according to a series of predetermined grades in the
    a. job classification system.
    b. job ranking method.
    c. point system.
    d. factor comparison method.

LO 3 _____ 15. A quantitative job evaluation procedure that determines the relative value of a job by the total points assigned to it is the
    a. points system.
    b. factor comparison method.
    c. job classification system.
    d. job ranking system.

LO 3 _____ 16. The point system of job evaluation requires the use of a
                         a. job specification.
                         b. job description.
                         c. job analysis.
                         d. points manual.

LO 3 _____ 17. A job evaluation system that has been developed specifically to evaluate executive, managerial, and professional positions is the
                         a. essay method.
                         b. forced-choice method.
                         c. critical incidents method.
                         d. Hay profile method.

LO 3 _____ 18. A job evaluation system that uses knowledge, mental activity, and accountability to evaluate positions is the
                         a. essay method.
                         b. forced-choice method.
                         c. critical incidents method.
                         d. Hay profile method.

LO 4 _____ 19. Job evaluation systems provide for internal equity and serve as the basis for
                         a. wage-rate determination.
                         b. performance appraisal.
                         c. job analysis.
                         d. comparable worth issues.

LO 4 _____ 20. A major national publisher of wage and salary data is the
                         a. Chamber of Commerce.
                         b. Bureau of Labor Statistics.
                         c. Internal Revenue Service.
                         d. Local Employer Association.

LO 5 _____ 21. The relationship between the relative worth of employees' jobs and their wage rates can be represented by means of a(n)
                         a. escalator clause.
                         b. comparable worth system.
                         c. wage curve.
                         d. job ranking system.

LO 5 _____ 22. Wages paid above the range maximum are called
                         a. competence-based pay.
                         b. comparable worth.
                         c. red circle rates.
                         d. wage-rate compression.

LO 5 _____ 23. The method that compensates employees for the different skills or increased knowledge they possess rather than for the job they hold in a designated job category is known as
  a. broadbanding.
  b. competence-based pay.
  c. job enlargement.
  d. pay-for-performance.

LO 6 _____ 24. Assessing the compensation program involves all of the following except
  a. ban the use of a compensation scorecard.
  b. help detect compensation problems.
  c. make compensation decisions more transparent.
  d. align compensation decisions with organizational objectives.

LO 7 _____ 25. The major provisions of the Fair Labor Standards Act include the following, *except*
  a. equal pay for equal work.
  b. minimum-wage rates.
  c. overtime payments.
  d. child labor.

LO 7 _____ 26. Which act is also referred to as the Prevailing Wage Law?
  a. Equal Pay Act.
  b. Davis-Bacon Act.
  c. Walsh-Healy Act.
  d. Fair Labor Standards Act.

LO 7 _____ 27. The concept in which jobs historically held exclusively by men and by women are considered equal in terms of value or worth to the employer is known as
  a. sexual harassment.
  b. job evaluation.
  c. comparable worth.
  d. external pay equity.

LO 7 _____ 28. The internal pay-equity concern that results in the reduction of differences between job classes is
  a. employee empowerment.
  b. job enlargement.
  c. job specification.
  d. pay-rate compression.

LO 7 _____ 29. Avoiding pay-rate compression, consider all of the following except
  a. use merit pay.
  b. do not do anything to create pay-rate compression even if the firm can no longer compete for the high value talent it needs.
  c. prepare high performers for promotion to higher paying jobs.
  d. design the pay structure to provide a wide spread between hourly and supervisory employees.

LO 7 _____ 30. Under certain conditions the following may be exempt from overtime provisions except
  a. skilled metal workers.
  b. administrative workers.
  c. outside sales people.
  d. executives.

True/False

Identify the following statements as True or False.

Learning Outcome (LO)

LO 1 _____ 1. Pay equity is achieved when the compensation received is unequal to the value of the work performed.

LO 1 _____ 2. Work performed in most private, public, and not-for-profit organizations has traditionally been compensated on a professionally contracted basis.

LO 1 _____ 3. Salaried employees are generally paid the same for each pay period, even though they occasionally may work more hours or fewer than the regular number of hours in a period.

LO 1 _____ 4. Managers and supervisors as well as a large number of white-collar employees are in the nonexempt category of pay structure.

LO 2 _____ 5. Economic conditions and competition faced by employers do not significantly affect the rates they are able to pay.

LO 2 _____ 6. The major external factors that influence wage rates include labor market conditions, area wage rates, cost of living, legal requirements, and the employer's ability to pay.

LO 2 _____ 7. The consumer price index (CPI) is based on prices of food, clothing, shelter, fuels, transportation fares, charges for medical services, and prices of other goods and services that people buy for day-to-day living.

121

LO 3 _____ 8. All job evaluation methods require the same consistent degree of managerial judgment.

LO 3 _____ 9. Job ranking can be done by a single individual who has a working knowledge of all jobs; however, it should never be done by a committee composed of management and employee representatives.

LO 3 _____ 10. The basic weakness of the job ranking system is that it does not provide a very refined measure of each job's worth.

LO 3 _____ 11. The principle advantage of the point system job evaluation technique is that it provides a more refined basis for making judgments than either the ranking or classification systems.

LO 3 _____ 12. The cornerstone for work valuation is that work should be valued relative to the business goals of the organization rather than by an internally applied points-factor job evaluation system.

LO 4 _____ 13. Many states conduct wage and salary surveys on either a municipal or county basis and make them available to the Internal Revenue Service.

LO 5 _____ 14. A wage curve may be constructed graphically by preparing a scattergram, which consists of a series of dots that represent the current inflation rates.

LO 5 _____ 15. From an administrative standpoint, it is generally preferable to group jobs into pay grades and to pay all jobs within a particular grade a different rate or rate range.

LO 5 _____ 16. Pay grades are groups of jobs within a particular class that are paid different rates.

LO 5 _____ 17. The final step in setting up a wage structure is to determine the appropriate pay grade into which each job should be placed on the basis of its evaluated worth.

LO 5 _____ 18. Broadbanding uses many traditional salary grades for employee compensation.

LO 6 _____ 19. The compensation scorecard collects and displays the results of all the measures that a company uses to monitor and compare compensation among internal departments or units.

LO 7 _____ 20. Under the Fair Labor Standards Act (FLSA), employers are not required to pay time-and-a-half wages for hours worked in excess of forty hours in any particular week.

LO 7 _____ 21. One of the most significant acts to protect employees against pay discrimination was the Equal Pay Act passed in 1963.

LO 7 _____ 22. As managers strive to reward employees in a fair manner, they must consider controls over labor costs, legal issues regarding male and female wage payments, and external pay-equity concerns.

LO 7 _____ 23. There are several causes for wage-rate compression, including job analysis, job evaluation, and performance appraisal.

LO 7 _____ 24. Wage-rate compression often occurs when organizations grant pay adjustments for lower-rated jobs without providing commensurate adjustments for occupations at the top of the job hierarchy.

LO 7 _____ 25. Identifying wage-rate compression and its causes is far simpler than implementing organizational policies to alleviate its effects.

Matching

Match each term with the proper definition.

Terms

a. broadbanding
b. competence-based pay
c. consumer price index (CPI)
d. escalator clauses
e. exempt employees
f. Hay profile method
g. hourly work
h. job classification system
i. job evaluation
j. job ranking system
k. nonexempt employees
l. pay equity

m. pay-for-performance
n. pay grades
o. piecework
p. point system
q. real wages
r. red circle rates
s. wage and salary survey
t. wage curve
u. pay-rate compression
v. work valuation

Definitions

_____ 1. curve in a scattergram representing the relationship between the relative worth of jobs and their wage rates.

_____ 2. quantitative job evaluation procedure that determines the relative value of a job by the total points assigned to it.

_____ 3. standard by which managers tie compensation to employee effort and performance.

_____ 4. collapses many traditional salary grades into a few wide salary bands.

_____ 5. clauses in labor agreements that provide for quarterly cost-of-living adjustment in wages, basing the adjustments on changes in the consumer price index.

_____ 6. an employee's perception that compensation received is equal to the value of the work performed.

_____ 7. compression of differentials between job classes, particularly the differential between hourly workers and their managers.

_____ 8. work paid on an hourly basis.

_____ 9. groups of jobs within a particular class that are paid the same rate or rate range.

_____ 10. work paid according to the number of units produced.

_____ 11. employees not covered by the overtime provisions of the Fair Labor Standards Act.

_____ 12. measure of the average change in prices over time in a fixed "market basket" of goods and services.

_____ 13. systematic process of determining the relative worth of jobs in order to establish which jobs should be paid more than others within an organization.

_____ 14. job evaluation technique using three factors—knowledge, mental activity, and accountability—to evaluate executive and managerial positions.

_____ 15. survey of the wages paid to employees of other employers in the surveying organization's relevant labor market.

_____ 16. wage increases larger than rises in the consumer price index; that is, the real earning power of wages.

_____ 17. simplest and oldest system of job evaluation by which jobs are arrayed on the basis of their relative worth.

_____ 18. pay based on an employee's skill level, the variety of skills possessed, or increased job knowledge of the employee.

_____ 19. employees covered by the overtime provisions of the Fair Labor Standards Act.

_____ 20. system of job evaluation in which jobs are classified and grouped according to a series of predetermined wage grades.

_____ 21. payment rates above the maximum of the pay range.

_____ 22. a job evaluation system that seeks to measure a job's worth through its value to the organization.

Internet Exercises

Is comparable worth a solution for teachers?
http://www.findarticles.com/p/articles/mi_m0MJG/is_3_3/ai_104835530.

How can the labor force accommodate older workers?
http://www.springerlink.com/content/qjp5p00v83708513/

How to Negotiate a Fair Compensation Package

Research the job market for compensation or salary ranges for a graduating student in the field of business.

Wages and fringe benefits are important issues to present to a prospective employer. To gain access to this type of information, visit the college placement office, local chamber of commerce, library, or Internet.

In negotiating a fair compensation package with an employer, you should understand your economic needs. Offer a salary range rather than an exact amount when a potential employer asks your starting salary requirements. Know your salary objectives and career goals when interviewing with an employer. Following the interview, have questions ready concerning salary objectives and career development opportunities. Utilize previous job experience as a bargaining tool for obtaining a higher starting salary. Apply your marketing knowledge to project a positive image in the interview.

SOLUTIONS

Multiple Choice:	True/False:	Matching:
1. b	1. False	1. t
2. a	2. False	2. p
3. c	3. True	3. m
4. c	4. False	4. a
5. d	5. False	5. d
6. a	6. False	6. l
7. c	7. True	7. u
8. c	8. False	8. g
9. b	9. False	9. n
10. a	10. True	10. o
11. d	11. True	11. e
12. b	12. True	12. c
13. c	13. False	13. i
14. a	14. False	14. f
15. a	15. False	15. s
16. d	16. False	16. q
17. d	17. True	17. j
18. d	18. False	18. b
19. a	19. True	19. k
20. b	20. False	20. h
21. c	21. True	21. r
22. c	22. False	22. v
23. b	23. False	
24. a	24. True	
25. a	25. True	
26. b		
27. c		
28. d		
29. b		
30. a		

False Statements Made True

1. Pay equity is achieved when the compensation received is **equal** to the value of the work performed.

2. Work performed in most private, public, and not-for-profit organizations has traditionally been compensated on **an hourly** basis.

4.   Managers and supervisors as well as a large number of white-collar employees are in the **exempt** category of pay structure.

5.   Economic conditions and competition faced by employers **significantly** affect the rates they are able to pay.

6.   The major external factors that influence wage rates include labor market conditions, area wage rates, cost of living, legal requirements, and **collective bargaining if the employer is unionized.**

8.   All job evaluation methods require **varying degrees** of managerial judgment.

9.   Job ranking can be done by a single individual who has a working knowledge of all jobs, **or by** a committee composed of management and employee representatives.

13.   Many states conduct wage and salary surveys on **local, regional, or national** organizations and make them available to **employers**.

14.   A wage curve may be constructed graphically by preparing a scattergram, which consists of a series of dots that represent the current **wage** rates.

15.   From an administrative standpoint, it is generally preferable to group jobs into pay grades and to pay all jobs within a particular grade **the same** rate or rate range.

16.   Pay grades are groups of jobs within a particular class that are paid **the same rate**.

18.   Broadbanding **collapses** many traditional salary grades **into a few wide salary bands**.

20.   Under the Fair Labor Standards Act, employers **are** required to pay time-and-a-half wages for hours worked in excess of forty hours in any particular week.

22.   As managers strive to reward employees in a fair manner, they must consider controls over labor costs, legal issues regarding male and female wage payments, and **internal** pay-equity concerns.

23.   There are several causes for wage-rate compression, including **the granting of union-negotiated across-the-board increases for hourly employees without granting corresponding wage differentials for managerial personnel, and the scarcity of applicants.**

CHAPTER 10

PAY-FOR-PERFORMANCE: INCENTIVE REWARDS

Compensation can be a significant source of motivation if at least part of it is tied directly to the employee's performance. Countless financial incentive systems have been developed over the years to motivate employees who occupy various levels within an organization and who perform different types of duties. Some of these systems have been successful, while others have not. The success of a particular system depends not so much on the formula for determining incentive payments, as on the existence of a favorable climate in which the system can operate. Success also depends on the degree to which the system has been tailored to the needs of the organization where it is to be used. Contributing to this success, furthermore, are the ways in which the system allows employees to participate, psychologically as well as financially, in the organization. A rather new form of compensation—the employee stock ownership plan (ESOP)—can be advantageous to employers and to employees.

LEARNING OUTCOMES

After studying this chapter, you should be able to

LEARNING OUTCOME 1	Know how to implement incentive programs.
LEARNING OUTCOME 2	Identify the different types of incentive programs and why they work.
LEARNING OUTCOME 3	Explain why merit raises may fail to motivate employees and discuss ways to increase their motivational value.
LEARNING OUTCOME 4	Indicate two specific ways to compensate salespeople.

LEARNING OUTCOME 5   Differentiate how gains may be shared with employees under the Scanlon and Improshare gainsharing systems.

LEARNING OUTCOME 6   Differentiate between profit sharing plans and explain advantages and disadvantages of these programs.

LEARNING OUTCOME 7   Describe the main types of ESOP plans and discuss the advantages of ESOPs to employers and employees.

CHAPTER SUMMARY RELATING TO LEARNING OUTCOMES

LEARNING OUTCOME   The success of an incentive pay plan depends on the organizational climate in which it must operate, employee confidence in it, and its suitability to employee and organizational needs. Importantly, employees must view their incentive pay as being equitable and related to their performance. Performance measures should be quantifiable, be easily understood, and bear a demonstrated relationship to organizational performance.

LEARNING OUTCOME 2   Piecework plans pay employees a given rate for each unit satisfactorily completed. Employers implement these plans when output is easily measured and when the production process is fairly standardized. Bonuses are incentive payments above base wages paid on either an individual or team basis. A bonus is offered to encourage employees to exert greater effort. Standard hour plans establish a standard time for job completion. An incentive is paid for finishing the job in less than the pre-established time. These plans are popular for jobs with a fixed time for completion.

LEARNING OUTCOME 3   Merit raises will not serve to motivate employees when they are seen as entitlements, which occurs when these raises are given yearly without regard to changes in employee performance. Merit raises are not motivational when they are given because of seniority or favoritism or when merit budgets are inadequate to sufficiently reward employee performance. To be motivational, merit raises must be such that employees see a clear relationship between pay and performance, and the salary increase must be large enough to exceed inflation and higher income taxes.

LEARNING OUTCOME   Salespeople may be compensated by a straight salary, a combination of salary and commission, salary plus bonus, or a commission only. Paying employees a straight salary allows them to focus on tasks other than sales, such as service and customer goodwill. A straight commission plan causes employees to emphasize sales goals. A combination of salary and commission or bonus provides the advantages of both the straight salary and the straight commission form of payments.

LEARNING OUTCOME 5   The Scanlon and Improshare gainsharing plans pay bonuses to employees unrelated to profit levels. Each of these plans encourages employees to maximize their performance and cooperation through suggestions offered to improve organizational performance. The Scanlon Plan pays an employee a bonus based on saved labor cost measured against the organization's sales value of production. The Improshare bonus is paid when employees increase production output above a given target level.

LEARNING OUTCOME 6   Profit sharing plans pay employees sums of money based on the organization's profits. Cash payments are made to eligible employees at specified times, normally yearly. The primary purpose of profit sharing is to provide employees with additional income through their participation in organizational achievement. Employee commitment to improved productivity, quality, and customer service will contribute to organizational success and, in turn, to their compensation. Profit sharing plans may not achieve their stated gains when employee performance is unrelated to organizational success or failure. This may occur because of economic conditions, other competition, or environmental conditions. Profit sharing plans can have a negative effect on employee morale when plans fail to consistently reward employees.

LEARNING OUTCOME 7   With an ESOP, each year the organization contributes stock or cash to buy stock that is then placed in an ESOP trust. The ESOP holds the stock for employees until they either retire or leave the company, at which time the stock is sold back to the company or through a brokerage firm. Employers receive tax benefits for qualified ESOPs; they also hope to receive their employees' commitment to organizational improvement. Employees, however, may lose their retirement income should the company fail or stock prices fall. Another drawback to ESOPs is that they are not guaranteed by any federal agency.

REVIEW QUESTIONS

Multiple Choice

Choose the letter of the word or phrase that best completes each statement.

Learning Outcome (LO)

LO 1 _____   1. A clear trend in strategic compensation management is the growth of
   a. traditional pay plans.
   b. incentive plans.
   c. obsolescent piece-rate systems.
   d. antiquated group incentive systems.

LO 1 _____   2. Managers believe that employees will assume ownership of their jobs, thereby improving their effort and overall job performance, by meshing
a. traditional pay plans with those of employer associations.
b. compensation with that of the competition.
c. compensation and organizational objectives.
d. compensation programs with those outside the industry.

LO 1 _____   3. The success of an incentive plan in an organization depends on
a. employee morale.
b. treating employees fairly.
c. harmony between employees and management.
d. all of the above.

LO 1 _____   4. Management should never allow incentive payments to be seen as
a. a bonus.
b. variable pay.
c. an entitlement.
d. a reward.

LO 2 _____   5. The following impact the organization's choice of incentive pay plans, *except*
a. technology.
b. job tasks and duties.
c. organizational goals.
d. social orientation.

LO 2 _____   6. One of the oldest incentive plans is based on
a. technology.
b. job tasks and duties.
c. organizational goals.
d. piecework.

LO 2 _____   7. Employees whose production exceeds the standard output receive a higher rate for all of their work than the rate paid to those who do not exceed the standard under a
a. holidays and vacations system.
b. differential piece-rate plan.
c. career curve method.
d. socialization process.

LO 2 _____   8. A plan that sets incentive rates on the basis of a predetermined standard time for completing a job is known as the
a. combined salary and commission plan.
b. piece-rate incentive plan.
c. standard hour plan.
d. street commission plan.

LO 2 _____ 9. An annual payment that is supplemental to the basic wage for employees is a
    a. contracted wage.
    b. fringe benefit.
    c. differential piece rate.
    d. bonus.

LO 2 _____ 10. A raise that links an increase in base pay to how successfully an employee performs his or her job is a
    a. merit pay program.
    b. combined salary and commission plan.
    c. piece rate plan.
    d. Scanlon Plan.

LO 3 _____ 11. One of the major weaknesses of merit raises lies in increases based on a
    a. performance appraisal system.
    b. differential piece rate.
    c. straight commission plan.
    d. competitive benchmarking plan.

LO 3 _____ 12. A method of pay in which employers receive a year-end merit payment that is not added to their base pay is called a
    a. combined salary and commission plan.
    b. lump-sum merit program.
    c. team incentive plan.
    d. gainsharing plan.

LO 4 _____ 13. A sales incentive plan that is based on a percentage of sales and provides maximum incentive for the salesperson is the
    a. straight salary plan.
    b. combined salary and commission plan.
    c. Scanlon Plan.
    d. straight commission plan.

LO 4 _____ 14. A cash advance which must be paid back as commissions are earned is called a
    a. bonus.
    b. draw.
    c. salary.
    d. lump sum.

LO 4 _____ 15. The most widely used sales incentive program is the
a. combined salary and commission plan.
b. straight commission plan.
c. lump-sum bonus.
d. annual bonus.

LO 4 _____ 16. Salespeople's performance may be measured by all of the following except
a. dollar volume of sales.
b. ability to establish new accounts.
c. ability to promote new products.
d. seasonal variations.

LO 4 _____ 17. Normally the only factor among the following that may be under the sales person's control is
a. economic fluctuations.
b. customer service.
c. competition.
d. changes in demand.

LO 4 _____ 18. The benefits of paying salespeople a straight salary include all of the following except
a. sales people may perform duties important to the firm that do not create revenue for the sales person.
b. provide services to customers.
c. might not engage in the extra effort to make a sale.
d. build goodwill for the firm.

LO 4 _____ 19. All of the following are limitations of a straight commission except
a. customer service after the sale may be neglected.
b. earnings fluctuate.
c. sales people may be tempted to grant price concessions.
d. motivation to sell more.

LO 4 _____ 20. Which of the following is not an advantage for the firm in a combination salary-and-commission plan?
a. recruiting sales people for management.
b. most favorable ratio of selling expense to sales.
c. motivation to achieve marketing objectives in addition to sales volume.
d. greater design flexibility.

LO 5 _____ 21. The Scanlon Plan emphasizes
    a. participative management.
    b. economic forecasts.
    c. supplemental pay benefits.
    d. competitive reactions.

LO 5 _____ 22. The type of bonus plan in which employees offer ideas and suggestions to improve productivity in the plant and are then rewarded for their constructive efforts is the
    a. annual bonus plan.
    b. Scanlon Plan.
    c. day-rate plan.
    d. combined salary and commission plan.

LO 5 _____ 23. Which of the following is an individual incentive plan?
    a. Scanlon Plan.
    b. Improshare.
    c. profit sharing plan.
    d. piecework.

LO 5 _____ 24. Which of the following is a group incentive plan?
    a. merit-pay.
    b. Improshare.
    c. profit sharing plan.
    d. piecework.

LO 5 _____ 25. Which of the following is an enterprise incentive plan?
    a. Scanlon Plan.
    b. Improshare.
    c. profit sharing plan.
    d. piecework.

LO 5 _____ 26. A gainsharing program based upon overall productivity of the work team is called a(n)
    a. competition benchmarking program.
    b. team incentive plan.
    c. earnings-at-risk incentive plan.
    d. Improshare plan.

LO 5 _____ 27. Common enterprise incentive plans include
    a. profit-sharing.
    b. stock options.
    c. employee stock ownership plans (ESOPs).
    d. all of the above.

LO 6 _____   28. Any procedure in which an employer pays all regular employees
special current or deferred sums based upon the profits of the enterprise is
a. a profit-sharing plan.
b. gainsharing.
c. a Scanlon plan.
d. a piece-rate plan.

LO 6 _____   29. An incentive plan that gives employees the opportunity to increase their
earnings by contributing to the growth of their organization's profits is
known as a
a. straight commission plan.
b. straight salary plan.
c. combined salary and commission plan.
d. profit-sharing plan.

LO 7 _____   30. The type of incentive that may take the form of a stock bonus plan or a
leveraged plan is the
a. employee stock ownership plan.
b. performance units.
c. Scanlon Plan.
d. combined salary and commission plan.

True/False

Identify the following statements as True or False.

Learning Outcome (LO)

LO 1 _____   1. Incentive plans always satisfy employee needs as well as the
organization's needs.

LO 1 _____   2. The primary purpose of an incentive compensation plan is to ensure that
employees have the opportunity to make some extra money under all
circumstances.

LO 2 _____   3. Straight piecework, one of the newest incentive plans is based on
piecework.

LO 2 _____   4. Straight piecework employees receive a varying rate of pay for each unit
produced.

LO 2 _____   5. One of the most significant weaknesses of piecework, as well as other
incentive plans based on individual effort, is that it may not always be an
effective motivator.

LO 2 _____   6. Piecework is appropriate where quality is more important than quantity.

LO 2 _____   7. Bonuses may be determined on the basis of cost reduction, quality improvement, or performance criteria established by the organization.

LO 3 _____   8. An advantage to receiving a single lump-sum merit payment is it can provide a clear link between pay and performance.

LO 3 _____   9. Research clearly shows that noncash incentive awards are most effective as motivators when the award is combined with a meaningful employee recognition program.

LO 5 _____   10. The Scanlon Plan emphasizes participative management.

LO 5 _____   11. Under the Scanlon Plan, financial incentives based on increases in employee productivity are not offered to all employees, only executives.

LO 5 _____   12. The Scanlon Plan is an individual incentive plan.

LO 5 _____   13. Profit sharing plans are based on the organization's stock price.

LO 5 _____   14. Improshare output is measured by the number of finished products that a work team produces in a given period.

LO 5 _____   15. Improshare is a bonus plan based on dollar savings much like the Scanlon Plan.

LO 5 _____   16. Enterprise incentive plans reward employees on the basis of the success of the organization over an extended period of time—normally one year, but the period can be longer.

LO 6 _____   17. The purpose of profit sharing is to have employees commit to a specific area of the organization.

LO 7 _____   18. Employee stock ownership programs (ESOPs) are more likely to serve their intended purposes in privately held companies than in publicly held ones.

LO 7 _____   19. Although studies show that productivity improves when employee stock ownership plans are implemented, these gains are not guaranteed.

LO 7 _____   20. Some organizations have extended the salary range for professional positions to equal or nearly equal that for administrative positions.

LO 7 _____   21. An analysis of executive salaries shows that the largest portion of executive pay is received in short-term incentive rewards and bonuses.

LO 7 _____ 22. Annual bonuses represent the main element of executive short-term incentives.

LO 7 _____ 23. Most organizations pay their short-term incentive bonuses in the form of common stock to maintain their pay-for-performance strategy.

LO 7 _____ 24. Balanced scorecards in terms of executive incentives are used to measure customer satisfaction, employee salary, and product or service leadership.

LO 7 _____ 25. Perquisites are nonmonetary rewards given to executives.

Matching

Match each term with the proper definition.

Terms

a. bonus
b. combined salary and commission plan
c. differential piece rate
d. employee stock ownership plans (ESOPs)
e. gainsharing plans
f. Improshare
g. lump-sum merit program
h. merit guidelines
i. perquisites
j. profit sharing

k. salary plus bonus plan
l. Scanlon Plan
m. spot bonus
n. standard hour plan
o. straight commission plan
p. straight piecework
q. straight salary plan
r. team incentive plan
s. variable pay

Definitions

_____ 1. gainsharing program under which bonuses are based on the overall productivity of the work team.

_____ 2. compensation plan based on a percentage of sales.

_____ 3. guidelines for awarding merit raises that are tied to performance objectives.

_____ 4. incentive payment that is supplemental to the base wage.

_____ 5. compensation plan that permits salespeople to be paid for performing various duties that are not reflected immediately in their sales volume.

_____ 6. compensation plan that pays a salary plus bonus achieved by reaching targeted sales goals.

_____ 7. stock plans in which an organization contributes shares of its stock to an established trust for the purpose of stock purchases by its employees.

_____ 8. unplanned bonus given for employee effort unrelated to an established performance measure.

_____ 9. compensation plan that includes a straight salary and a commission.

_____ 10. special nonmonetary benefits often given to executives.

_____ 11. programs under which both employees and the organization share the financial gains according to a predetermined formula that reflects improved productivity and profitability.

_____ 12. compensation rate under which employees whose production exceeds the standard amount of output receive a higher rate for all of their work than the rate paid to those who do not exceed the standard amount.

_____ 13. compensation plan in which all team members receive an incentive bonus payment when production or service standards are met or exceeded.

_____ 14. incentive plan that sets rates based on the completion of a job in a predetermined standard time.

_____ 15. program under which employees receive a year-end merit payment that is not added to their base pay.

_____ 16. bonus incentive plan using employee and management committees to gain cost-reduction improvements.

_____ 17. any procedure by which an employer pays or makes available to all regular employees, in addition to base pay, special current or deferred sums based on the profits of the enterprise.

_____ 18. incentive plan under which employees receive a certain rate for each unit produced.

_____ 19. tying pay to some measure of individual, group, or organizational performance.

Internet Exercises

How can an employer reward loyal employees?
http://www.findarticles.com/p/articles/mi_m0DTI/is_4_32/ai_n6038412.

What is the relationship between profit-sharing and gainsharing plans?
http://www.findarticles.com/p/articles/mi_m0OGT/is_1_3/ai_n8690365.

How to Motivate Student Behavior

Motivation can be defined in terms of behavior. Students who are motivated exhibit a greater effort to perform a task than do those who are not motivated. Essentially, motivation is the willingness to do something, which is conditioned by the ability to satisfy some need for the student. For instance, the amount of effort a student puts into a class determines whether he or she will pass or fail. There are different theories that explain how student behavior is motivated. The expectancy theory proposes that motivation depends on how much a student wants something and how likely he or she thinks it is that the item will be received. If a student perceives that studying and researching will lead to a specific outcome, such as a good grade or a career goal, then he or she is motivated to perform the needed tasks.

Another theory of motivation for student behavior is Maslow's needs hierarchy theory. This theory states that there are five needs ranked in a hierarchical order from lowest to highest. These needs are physiological, safety, belonging, esteem, and self-actualization. A student has to satisfy the lower-level needs in order to move up through the hierarchy. A student who is motivated to excel in academics is attempting to satisfy the esteem and self-actualization needs. If the lower-level needs are not met, the student will experience difficulty in being motivated to perform well in his or her studies.

SOLUTIONS

Multiple Choice:	**True/False:**	**Matching:**
1. b	1. False	1. f
2. c	2. False	2. o
3. d	3. False	3. h
4. c	4. False	4. a
5. d	5. True	5. q
6. d	6. False	6. k
7. b	7. True	7. d
8. c	8. True	8. m
9. d	9. True	9. b
10. a	10. True	10. i
11. a	11. False	11. e
12. b	12. True	12. c

13.	d	13.	False	13.	r
14.	b	14.	False	14.	n
15.	a	15.	True	15.	g
16.	d	16.	True	16.	l
17.	b	17.	False	17.	j
18.	c	18.	False	18.	p
19.	d	19.	False	19.	s
20.	a	20.	True		
21.	a	21.	False		
22.	b	22.	True		
23.	d	23.	False		
24.	b	24.	False		
25.	c	25.	True		
26.	d				
27.	d				
28.	a				
29.	d				
30.	a				

False Statements Made True

1. Incentive plans **sometimes fail to** satisfy employee needs as well as the organization's needs.

2. The primary **purposes** of an incentive compensation plan **are measurement and rewards**.

3. Straight piecework, one of the **oldest** incentive plans is based on piecework.

4. Straight piecework employees receive a **certain** rate of pay for each unit produced.

6. Piecework is **inappropriate** where quality is more important than quantity.

11. Under the Scanlon Plan, financial incentives based on increases in employee productivity **are offered to all hourly employees**.

12. The Scanlon Plan is a **group** incentive plan.

13. Profit sharing plans are based on an organization's **profits**.

15. Improshare is a bonus plan **not** based on dollar savings **but on productivity gains that result from reducing production time**.

17. The purpose of profit sharing is to **motivate a total commitment from employees rather than having them** commit to a specific area of the organization.

18. Employee stock ownership programs (ESOPs) are more likely to serve their intended purposes in **publicly** held companies than in **privately** held ones.

21. An analysis of executive salaries shows that the largest portion of executive pay is received in **long-term** incentive rewards and bonuses.

23. Most organizations pay their short-term incentive bonuses in the form of **annual profit plans, payments based on performance rating, and/or achievement of goals**.

24. Balanced scorecards in terms of executive incentives are used to measure customer satisfaction, the **ability to innovate**, and product or service leadership.

CHAPTER 11

EMPLOYEE BENEFITS

A growing portion of the compensation employees receive is not provided in their paycheck. Rather, it is paid in the form of benefits that employers increasingly must offer to compete in the labor market or to satisfy union demands or legal requirements. In order to emphasize that these benefits constitute a significant part of the compensation employees are paid, employers increasingly are using the term "total compensation." Different types of employee benefits entail different problems and costs.

LEARNING OUTCOMES

After studying this chapter, you should be able to

LEARNING OUTCOME 1   Explain why companies offer their employee's benefits and are concerned about their costs.

LEARNING OUTCOME 2   Describe the elements that have to be considered when developing a strategic benefits plan.

LEARNING OUTCOME 3   Identify and explain the employee benefits required by law.

LEARNING OUTCOME 4   Discuss the strategies companies utilize to control the costs of employee health care programs.

LEARNING OUTCOME 5   Describe benefits that involve payment for time not worked.

LEARNING OUTCOME 6   Discuss the recent trends in retirement policies and programs.

LEARNING OUTCOME 7   Describe the different types of pension plans employers offer and the regulations related to them.

LEARNING OUTCOME 8   Describe the types of work/life benefits that employers may provide.

CHAPTER SUMMARY RELATING TO LEARNING OUTCOMES

LEARNING OUTCOME 1   Employee benefits were not always the norm in America. The situation changed in 1935 with the passage of the Social Security Act. However, benefits can add 30–40 percent or more to a company's payroll costs, and they continue to climb faster than the rate of inflation. As a result, firms look closely at their benefit costs.

LEARNING OUTCOME 2   A variety of factors need to be considered when designing a strategic benefits plan. Included among them are the relative preference shown for each benefit by managers and employees, the estimated cost of each benefit and the total amount of money available for the entire benefits package, and how it compares to the competition. Through committees and surveys, a benefits package can be developed to meet employees' needs. Through the use of flexible benefit, or cafeteria, plans, employees are able to choose the benefits that are best suited for their individual needs. An important factor in how employees view the program is the full communication of benefits information through various means and personalized benefits statements. Online systems have also helped with the communication process and made it easier for HR departments to administer employee benefits.

LEARNING OUTCOME 3   Nearly a quarter of the benefits package that employers provide is legally required. These benefits include employer contributions to Social Security, unemployment insurance, workers' compensation insurance, and state disability insurance. Social Security taxes collected from employers and employees are used to pay three major types of benefits: (1) retirement benefits, (2) disability benefits, and (3) survivors' benefits. Payroll deductions and taxes are also legally required to fund the government program, Medicare. Medicare provides medical and hospital insurance and prescription drug coverage for people over 65.

LEARNING OUTCOME   The cost of healthcare programs has become the major concern in the area of employee benefits. Organizations are taking a variety of approaches to contain health care costs. They include using health maintenance and preferred provider organizations and high-deductible health plans as well as reducing employees' coverage and increasing their deductibles or copayments. Employee assistance programs, disease management and wellness programs, disease management and wellness programs, and value-based initiatives that target the specific health needs of an employer's workers are other approaches.

LEARNING OUTCOME 5   Included in the category of benefits that involve payments for time not worked are vacations with pay, paid holidays, sick leave, and severance pay. Some companies offer their employees paid sabbaticals. A typical practice in the United States is to give ten days' vacation leave and ten holidays. In addition to vacation time, most employees, particularly in white-collar jobs, receive a set number of sick-leave days. A one-time payment of severance pay may be given to employees who are being terminated.

LEARNING OUTCOME 6   For most professions in the United States, there is no mandatory retirement age. The topics covered can include pension plans, health insurance coverage, Social Security and Medicare, personal financial planning, wellness and lifestyles, and the general process of adjusting to retirement.

LEARNING OUTCOME 7   Whether to offer a pension plan is the employer's prerogative. However, once a plan is established it is then subject to federal regulation under ERISA to ensure that benefits will be available when an employee retires. Two pension plans are available – defined benefit and defined contribution. With a defined-benefit plan, the amount an employee receives on retirement is based on years of service, average earnings, and age at time of retirement. Two of the most significant trends are the growth of 401(k) plans and cash-balance pension plans, both of which are defined contribution plans. A concern today is the underfunding of pension plans and the ability of PGCA to meet its financial obligations.

LEARNING OUTCOME   The types of service benefits that employers typically provide include employee assistance programs, counseling services, educational assistance plans, child care, and elder care. Other benefits are food services, on-site health services, prepaid legal services, financial planning, housing and moving, transportation pooling, purchase assistance, credit unions, and social and recreational services.

REVIEW QUESTIONS

Multiple Choice

Choose the letter of the word or phrase that best completes each statement.

Learning Outcome (LO)

LO 1 _____   1. What is the relationship between total benefits and total compensation?
a. None. Compensation refers only to the paycheck.
b. Can represent 40% of total compensation.
c. benefits normally exceed wages and salaries.
d. government has taken over most benefit programs.

LO 1 _____   2. Which is true regarding benefits?
a. Firms provide only those benefits that they are forced by the government to provide.
b. Job applicants are interested only in the cash they get each payday, not some benefit they may or may not ever need.
c. Many firms offer benefits voluntarily, not just the benefits that are legally required.
d. a and b above.

LO 2 _____   3. In managing an employee benefits program, management must consider the following, *except*
a. union demands.
b. benefits other employers are offering.
c. reengineering programs.
d. tax consequences.

LO 2 _____   4. In designing an employee benefits program, management should
    a. allow for employee involvement.
    b. provide flexible benefits for a diverse work force.
    c. a and b above.
    d. use its own good judgment in establishing a standard benefit package for all.

LO 3 _____   5. Under the social security program, a fully insured person has earned
    a. 40 credits.
    b. 50 credits.
    c. 60 credits.
    d. 100 credits.

LO 3 _____   6. How many workweeks of unpaid leave can an eligible employee take in a 12-month period under FMLA?
    a. 10 weeks.
    b. 12 weeks.
    c. 14 weeks.
    d. 16 weeks.

LO 3 _____   7. An act that provides an insurance plan designed to protect covered individuals against loss of earnings resulting from various causes is the
    a. Equal Pay Act.
    b. Social Security Act.
    c. Civil Rights Act.
    d. Employee Retirement Income Security Act.

LO 3 _____   8. Individual employees should not be required to bear the cost of their treatment or loss of income, nor should they be subjected to complicated, delaying, and expensive legal procedures under
    a. workers' compensation insurance.
    b. life insurance.
    c. health insurance.
    d. prescription optical insurance.

LO 3 _____   9. Groups that offer routine medical services at a specific site for a fixed fee for each employee visit are called
    a. prescription drug services.
    b. rehabilitation services.
    c. health maintenance organizations.
    d. dental plans.

LO 3 _____ 10. As to the 2010 legislation involving new mandates upon business regarding health care, employers seem to be most concerned about being forced to
    a. cover employees' children up to age 26.
    b. cover those who only work 30 hours a week.
    c. both of the above.
    d. none of the above.

LO 3 _____ 11. A preferred provider organization is
    a. a group of physicians who form an organization or network.
    b. a guaranty of lower costs to employers.
    c. one that uses controls resulting in less diagnostic tests.
    d. all of the above.

LO 3 _____ 12. The act that grants employees the right to switch their medical insurance between former and present employers is the
    a. Occupational Safety and Health Act (OSHA).
    b. Credit Reporting Act.
    c. Employee Retirement Income and Security Act (ERISA).
    d. Health Insurance Portability and Accountability Act (HIPAA).

LO 4 _____ 13. Some companies waive deductibles and copays for employees who travel overseas to
    a. improve their health by climbing, swimming, and hiking.
    b. attend health seminars.
    c. obtain less expensive medical care.
    d. a and b above.

LO 4 _____ 14. Which are examples of wellness programs provided by some employers?
    a. personal trainers.
    b. nutrition counselors.
    c. treadmill desks.
    d. all of the above.

LO 4 _____ 15. To help workers cope with a wide variety of problems that interfere with job performance, organizations have developed
    a. employee assistance programs.
    b. 401(k) plans.
    c. severance pay packages.
    d. contributory plans.

LO 5 _____   16. The category of benefits that includes paid vacations, bonuses given in lieu of paid vacations, payments for holidays not worked, paid sick leave, military and jury duty, and payments for absence due to a death in the family or other personal reasons is called
   a. unemployment insurance.
   b. payment for time not worked.
   c. Social Security insurance.
   d. payment for time worked.

LO 5 _____   17. A one-time payment, usually dependent on an individual's years of service that is given to employees who are being terminated is
   a. unemployment insurance.
   b. supplemental unemployment benefits (SUBs).
   c. vacation pay.
   d. severance pay.

LO 5 _____   18. Insurance designed to pay for nursing home and other medical costs during old age is known as
   a. long-term care insurance.
   b. prescription optical insurance.
   c. prescription drug insurance.
   d. workers' compensation insurance.

LO 6 _____   19. Mandatory retirement is required for
   a. all people over the age of 70.
   b. airline pilots at age 65.
   c. both of the above.
   d. none of the above.

LO 6 _____   20. Polaroid's "retirement rehearsal" consists of
   a. practice for a formal retirement ceremony.
   b. coming to work late and leaving early.
   c. three months of unpaid leave.
   d. none of the above.

LO 7 _____   21. The type of pension plan in which the amount an employee is to receive upon retirement is specifically set forth is the
   a. voluntary fringe plan.
   b. noncontributory holiday plan.
   c. involuntary benefit plan.
   d. defined-benefit plan.

LO 7 _____ 22. The type of pension plan in which contributions are jointly made by employers and employees is a/an
a. voluntary fringe plan.
b. noncontributory holiday plan.
c. involuntary benefit plan.
d. contributory plan.

LO 7 _____ 23. A tax-deferred plan that allows employees to save through payroll deductions and to have their contributions matched by the employer is known as
a. supplemental unemployment benefits (SUBs).
b. unemployment insurance.
c. a 401(k) savings plan.
d. Social Security insurance.

LO 7 _____ 24. A guarantee of accrued benefits to participants at retirement age, regardless of their employment status at the time, is known as
a. portability.
b. vestibule training.
c. piece rate.
d. vesting.

LO 7 _____ 25. Private pension plans are subject to federal regulation under the
a. National Labor Relations Act.
b. Employee Retirement Income Security Act (ERISA).
c. National Industry Recovery Act.
d. Truth and Lending Law.

LO 7 _____ 26. With a diverse workforce, an increasing number of employers are willing to provide benefits to employees who establish
a. domestic partnership.
b. health maintenance organizations (HMOs).
c. human resources plans.
d. employee vesting.

LO 7 _____ 27. The following are standards that enable an employee to qualify under a domestic partnership in an organization, *except*
a. minimum age requirement.
b. specification of financial independence.
c. requirement that the couple live together.
d. requirement that the relationship be a permanent one.

LO 8 _____   28. The benefit provided to an older relative by an employee who remains
                        actively at work is called
                        a. elder care.
                        b. dental insurance.
                        c. life insurance.
                        d. health insurance.

LO 8 _____   29. To reduce the negative effects of caregiving on productivity,
                        organizations may offer
                        a. elder care seminars.
                        b. elder care support groups.
                        c. leaves of absence for elder care.
                        d. all of the above.

LO 8 _____   30. Which of the following programs are seen as a hedge against talent drain
                        and also as encouraging employee retention?
                        a. retirement planning.
                        b. tax planning and management.
                        c. estate planning.
                        d. educational assistance

True/False

Identify the following statements as True or False.

Learning Outcome (LO)

LO 1 _____   1. Like any other component of the human resources program, an employee
                       benefits program should be based on specific objectives.

LO 1 _____   2. Before a new benefit is introduced, the need for it should first be
                       determined through a consultation with customers.

LO 1 _____   3. To accommodate the individual needs of employees, there is a trend
                       toward flexible benefits plans, also known as cafeteria plans.

LO 2 _____   4. Since many benefits represent a variable rather than a fixed cost,
                       management must decide whether or not it can afford this cost under less
                       favorable economic conditions.

LO 2 _____   5. Legally required employee benefits constitute nearly a quarter of the
                       benefits package that employers provide.

LO 3 _____ 6. To be eligible for old-age and survivors' insurance as well as for disability and unemployment insurance under the Social Security Act, an individual need not be engaged in employment covered by the act.

LO 3 _____ 7. Workers' compensation laws typically provide that employees will be paid a disability benefit based on work performance.

LO 3 _____ 8. A covered employer must grant an eligible employee up to a total of two workweeks of unpaid leave in a two-month period under the Family and Medical Leave Act.

LO 4 _____ 9. The approaches used to contain the costs of health care benefits include reductions in coverage, increased deductibles or co-payments, and increased coordination of benefits.

LO 4 _____ 10. The preferred provider organization (PPO) is a group of physicians who establish an organization through lower service charges or agreed-upon utilization controls.

LO 4 _____ 11. Companies do not provide any benefits for people to obtain health care overseas.

LO 5 _____ 12. Although not required by law, employers in cyclical industries provide supplemental unemployment benefits.

LO 5 _____ 13. One of the oldest and most popular employee benefits is group term life insurance, which provides death benefits to beneficiaries and may also provide accidental death and dismemberment benefits.

LO 6 _____ 14. Phased retirement programs can help organizations with the "brain drain."

LO 6 _____ 15. As more baby-boomers continue to work, the number of phased retirement programs is expected to decline.

LO 7 _____ 16. In a contributory plan, contributions are made solely by the employer.

LO 7 _____ 17. When pension plans are classified by the amount of pension benefits to be paid, there are two basic types: the defined-benefit plan and the defined-contribution plan.

LO 7 _____ 18. Unlike traditional defined-benefit pension plans which guarantee payments based on years of service, the 401(k) plans guarantee nothing.

LO 7 _____ 19. An employer can revoke vested pension benefits that have been earned by an employee.

LO 7 _____ 20. Managers and supervisors should remember that antidiscrimination laws apply to the administration of benefit programs.

LO 7 _____ 21. Organizations that offer benefits to domestic partners are simply extending current benefits, normally full medical and dental plans, to employees.

LO 8 _____ 22. The increased employment of women with dependent children has created an unprecedented demand for childcare arrangements.

LO 8 _____ 23. Demand for elder care programs will decrease dramatically as baby boomers move into their fifties and find themselves managing organizations.

LO 8 _____ 24. Although the employer may provide office space and a payroll deduction service, employee services such as the use of credit unions are operated by the employees under federal and state legislation and supervision.

LO 8 _____ 25. Many organizations do not offer some type of sports program in which personnel may participate on a voluntary basis.

Matching

Match each term with the proper definition.

Terms

a.   backup care program
b.   contributory plan
c.   defined-benefit plan
d.   defined-contribution plan
e.   disease management programs
f.   elder care
g.   employee assistance program (EAP)
h.   flexible benefits plans (cafeteria plans)
i.   health maintenance organizations (HMO)
j.   high-deductible health plans (HDHP)
k.   noncontributory plan
l.   phased retirement
m.   preferred provider organization (PPO)
n.   sabbatical
o.   severance pay
p.   supplemental unemployment benefits (SUBs)
q.   vesting
r.   wellness programs
s.   workers' compensation insurance

Definitions

_____ 1. benefit plans that enable individual employees to choose the benefits that are best suited to their particular needs.

_____ 2. a guarantee of accrued benefits to participants at retirement age, regardless of their employment status at that time.

_____ 3. organizations of physicians and health care professionals that provide a wide range of services to subscribers and dependents on a prepaid basis.

_____ 4. care provided to an elderly relative by an employee who remains actively at work.

_____ 5. federal- or state-mandated insurance provided to workers to defray the loss of income and cost of treatment due to work-related injuries or illness.

_____ 6. a pension plan in which contributions are made jointly by employees and employers.

_____ 7. a pension plan in which contributions are made solely by the employer.

_____ 8. services provided by employers to help workers cope with a wide variety of problems that interfere with the way they perform their jobs.

_____ 9. a plan that enables an employee who is laid off to draw weekly benefits, in addition to state unemployment compensation, from the employer that are paid from a fund created for this purpose.

_____ 10. a pension plan in which the amount an employee is to receive upon retirement is specifically set forth.

_____ 11. non-contributory plan phased retirement.

_____ 12. a pension plan that establishes the basis on which an employer will contribute to the pension fund.

_____ 13. a group of physicians who establish an organization that guarantees lower health care costs to the employer.

_____ 14. a benefit program whereby an employer provides or subsidizes temporary care for its employee's elders or children when their regular arrangements fall through.

_____ 15. programs that provide patients and their caregivers with information on monitoring and treating medical conditions, while coordinating communication between them, their health care providers, employers, and insurers.

_____ 16. a program that allows its employees to gradually cut their hours before retiring.

_____ 17. paid (or unpaid) time away from a job for four or more weeks employees take off to renew themselves before returning to work.

_____ 18. a one-time payment sometimes given to an employee who is being involuntarily terminated.

_____ 19. employer-sponsored programs designed to encourage employees to maintain and improve their health and well-being by getting regular checkups, eating properly, exercising, and managing their stress levels so as to prevent costly and protracted illnesses.

Internet Exercise

What are the benefits of cafeteria plans?
http://www.entrepreneur.com/humanresources/compensationandbenefits/article79978.html

How to Recognize the Importance of Fringe Benefits

Employee benefits generally comprise various rewards, incentives, and other rights of value that an organization provides to its employees beyond their wages, salaries, and other forms of direct financial compensation. A benefits program should be more than a laundry list of specific entitlements. It should be a well-developed package of benefits and benefit options that best fulfill the needs of employees and the organization.

There are several types of fringe benefits offered by employers. Laws mandate that all employees must have certain benefits such as Social Security, unemployment insurance, and worker's compensation. Other benefits include health and dental plans, private pension plans, and paid time off in the form of vacation time, holiday pay, sick leave, and personal time. Employers have also included in their benefits package wellness programs, child care, elder care, and employee assistance programs.

Probably the most important option is health care coverage. While law does not mandate this benefit, it has become standard. With the increasing cost of health care and the rise of managed care, this benefit has been a major concern for employees. The ideal plan is one in which the employer gives the employee options and pays for a significant portion of the costs.

A popular type of benefit package is a cafeteria-style plan. This often is the best alternative because it allows employees to choose the benefits they really want. Employees are given a list of benefits and costs, and they can choose any combination that best serves their needs. This has become increasingly important with the rise of two-income families. One spouse may have a better health plan with an employer. This plan would allow the other spouse to elect another benefit option and reduce the costs. It also provides flexibility in the benefit selection process. Employees should analyze the benefit options offered by potential employers, and weigh the employment decision accordingly.

SOLUTIONS

Multiple Choice:		True/False:		Matching:	
1.	b	1.	True	1.	h
2.	c	2.	False	2.	q
3.	c	3.	True	3.	i
4.	c	4.	False	4.	f
5.	a	5.	True	5.	s
6.	b	6.	False	6.	b
7.	b	7.	False	7.	k
8.	a	8.	False	8.	g
9.	c	9.	True	9.	p
10.	c	10.	True	10.	c
11.	d	11.	False	11.	j
12.	d	12.	True	12.	d
13.	c	13.	False	13.	m
14.	d	14.	True	14.	a
15.	a	15.	False	15.	e
16.	b	16.	False	16.	l
17.	d	17.	True	17.	n
18.	a	18.	True	18.	o
19.	b	19.	False	19.	r
20.	c	20.	True		
21.	d	21.	True		
22.	d	22	True		
23.	c	23.	False		
24.	d	24.	True		
25.	b	25.	False		
26.	a				
27.	b				
28.	a				
29.	d				
30.	d				

False Statements Made True

2. Before a new benefit is introduced, the need for it should first be determined through a consultation with **employees**.

4. Since many benefits represent a **fixed** rather than a **variable** cost, management must decide   whether or not it can afford this cost under less favorable economic conditions.

6. To be eligible for old-age and survivors' insurance as well as for disability and unemployment insurance under the Social Security Act, an individual **must** be engaged in employment covered by the act.

7. Workers' compensation laws typically provide that employees will be paid a disability benefit based on **a percentage of their wages**.

8. A covered employer must grant an eligible employee up to a total of **twelve** workweeks of unpaid leave in a **twelve**-month period under the Family and Medical Leave Act.

11. Companies do provide benefits **(waiving deductibles and copays)** for people to obtain health care overseas **if it less expensive than in the U.S.**

15. As more baby-boomers continue to work, the number of phased retirement programs is expected to **increase.**

16. In a **noncontributory** plan, contributions are made solely by the employer.

19. An employer **cannot** revoke vested pension benefits that have been earned by an employee.

23. Demand for elder care programs will **increase** dramatically as baby boomers move into their fifties and find themselves managing organizations.

25. Many organizations **do offer** some type of sports program in which personnel may participate on a voluntary basis.

CHAPTER 12

PROMOTING SAFETY AND HEALTH

Safety and health programs have continued to receive employer attention since the passage of the Occupational Safety and Health Act (OSHA). For several reasons discussed in the text, employers have intensified their efforts to create safe work environments. Similarly, they have developed programs to reduce health hazards on the job. Many employers have instituted programs for building better health and for providing assistance to employees. They have developed stress-management programs to teach employees how to minimize the negative effects of job-related stress.

LEARNING OUTCOMES

After studying this chapter, you should be able to

LEARNING OUTCOME 1	Summarize the general provisions of the Occupational Safety and Health Act (OSHA).
LEARNING OUTCOME 2	Describe the measures managers and employees can take to create a safe work environment.
LEARNING OUTCOME 3	Identify ways to control and eliminate various on-the-job health hazards.
LEARNING OUTCOME 4	Describe the programs organizations utilize to build better health among their workforces.
LEARNING OUTCOME 5	Indicate the methods for coping with job stress.

CHAPTER SUMMARY RELATING TO LEARNING OUTCOMES

LEARNING OUTCOME   The Occupational Safety and Health Act was designed to assure, so far as possible, safe and healthful working conditions for every working person. In general, the act extends to all employers and employees. The Occupational Safety and Health Administration (OSHA) sets health and safety standards, ensures employers and employees comply with them, and provides safety and health consultation and training where needed. Both employers and employees have certain responsibilities and rights under OSHA. Employers not only are required to provide a hazard-free work environment, but also must keep employees informed about the OSHA requirements and provide them with protective equipment when necessary and ensure they wear it. Under the "right to know" regulations, employers are required to keep employees informed of hazardous substances and instruct them in avoiding the dangers presented. Employees, in turn, are required to comply with the OSHA standards, to report hazardous conditions, and to follow all employer safety and health regulations.

LEARNING OUTCOME 2   To provide safe working conditions for their employees, employers typically establish a formal safety program in liaison with their HR departments. The program may have many facets, including providing safety knowledge and motivating employees to use it, making employees aware of the need for safety, and rewarding them for safe behavior. Incentives such as praise, public recognition, and awards are used to involve employees in the safety program. Employers also engage their workers by asking them to join safety committees, help develop safety procedures, observe the safety practices of their coworkers, and investigate any accidents. The maintenance of required records from accident investigations provides a basis for information that can be used to create a safer work environment.

LEARNING OUTCOME 3   Job conditions that are dangerous to the health of employees are now receiving much greater attention than in the past. There is special concern for toxic chemicals that proliferate at a rapid rate and may lurk in the body for years without outward symptoms. Health hazards other than those found in manufacturing operations—such as video display terminals and cumulative trauma disorders—present special problems many firms are addressing with ergonomic solutions. Secondhand smoke and bloodborne pathogens are two other health hazards that have received greater attention in recent years.

LEARNING OUTCOME   Along with providing safer and healthier work environments, many employers establish programs that encourage employees to improve their health habits. Wellness programs that emphasize exercise, nutrition, weight control, and avoidance of harmful substances serve employees at all organizational levels. Alternative medicine approaches such as relaxation techniques and hypnosis, chiropractic care, acupuncture, homeopathy, herbal therapy, special diets, massage, and so forth are also used to help employees with a variety of health problems.

157

Managing Human Resources

LEARNING OUTCOME 5 An important dimension to health and safety is stress that comes from physical activity and mental or emotional activity. Many sources of stress are job related. Employers can develop stress management programs to help employees learn techniques for coping with stress. In addition, organizations need to redesign and enrich jobs, clarify the employee's work role, correct physical factors in the environment, and take any other actions that will help reduce stress on the job. Unchecked, stress can lead to depression, alcoholism, and drug abuse, which if severe enough, can be regarded as disabilities under the Americans with Disabilities Act. Managers need to be aware of the signs of these diseases and be prepared to help employees via EAPs or counseling and by making reasonable accommodations for the employees' treatment.

REVIEW QUESTIONS

Multiple Choice

Choose the letter of the word or phrase that best completes each statement.

Learning Outcome (LO)

LO 1 _____ 1. The act that has been very effective in reducing the number of injuries resulting in lost work time, the incident rate of specific injuries, and the number of job-related deaths is the
    a. Equal Pay Act.
    b. Age Discrimination and Employment Act.
    c. Occupational Safety and Health Act (OSHA).
    d. Pregnancy Leave Act.

LO 1 _____ 2. One of the responsibilities of the Occupational Safety and Health Administration is to develop and enforce
    a. mandatory pregnancy sick days.
    b. mandatory job safety and health standards.
    c. equal pay for equal work.
    d. nondiscriminatory applications pertaining to age requirements.

LO 1 _____ 3. The Occupational Safety and Health Administration can cite an employer for any of the following types of violations, *except*
    a. discipline procedure violations.
    b. other-than-serious violations.
    c. serious violations.
    d. willful violations.

LO 1 _____ 4. The Occupational Safety and Health Administration may propose penalties of up to $70,000 for each act of which type of violation?
a. discipline procedure violations.
b. other-than-serious violations.
c. serious violations.
d. willful violations.

LO 1 _____ 5. The government agency that provides a free on-site safety consultation service is the
a. Federal Trail Commission.
b. Occupational Safety and Health Administration.
c. Food and Drug Administration.
d. National Labor Relations Board.

LO 1 _____ 6. Which cooperative program provides recognition to employers who demonstrate exemplary achievement in workplace health and safety?
a. voluntary retirement programs.
b. employer associations.
c. affirmative action programs.
d. safety and health achievement recognition program.

LO 1 _____ 7. The definition of toxic and hazardous substances, the duties of employers and manufacturers to provide health-risk information to employees, trade-secret protection, and enforcement provisions are statutes addressed under
a. pregnancy leave.
b. employee right-to-know laws.
c. business necessity actions.
d. bona fide occupational qualifications.

LO 2 _____ 8. The most important purpose of a safety awareness program is to promote awareness of safety considerations among the following people in an organization, *except*
a. customers.
b. managers.
c. supervisors.
d. subordinates.

LO 2 _____ 9. Many organizations cover first aid, defensive driving, accident prevention techniques, handling of hazardous materials, and emergency procedures in their
a. affirmative action policy.
b. safety and health training.
c. business ethics code.
d. mission statement.

LO 2 _____ 10. Computer training techniques to enhance safety awareness would include the following, *except*
   a. e-tools.
   b. interactive CD-ROMs.
   c. Local Area Networks.
   d. PowerPoint presentations.

LO 2 _____ 11. Specific rules and regulations concerning safety are communicated through
   a. bulletin board notices.
   b. employee handbooks.
   c. signs attached to equipment.
   d. all of the above.

LO 2 _____ 12. A recordable case is any injury or illness that results in any of the following, *except*
   a. death.
   b. days away from work.
   c. restricted work or transfer to another job.
   d. vacation.

LO 3 _____ 13. The U.S. Supreme in the *Johnson Controls (1991)* case ruled that employers may not
   a. bar women from certain jobs due to risk of sexual harassment.
   b. bar women of childbearing age from certain jobs because of potential risk to their fetuses.
   c. bar women from bringing their children to work on Sundays.
   d. reduce indoor air quality on holidays.

LO 3 _____ 14. Mini-breaks that involve exercises, properly designed workstations, the changing of positions, and improvement in tool design are ways an organization can prevent
   a. sexual harassment.
   b. chemical hazards.
   c. cumulative trauma disorders.
   d. indoor air quality.

LO 3 _____ 15. Means of lessening health hazards include all of the following *except*
   a. substituting materials.
   b. unaltered processes.
   c. issuing protective equipment.
   d. improving ventilation.

LO 3 _____ 16. Key elements for a successful ergonomics program include all of the following *except*
a. provide employee training.
b. use experts instead of employee participation.
c. conduct preinjury hazard assessment.
d. file injury reports.

LO 3 _____ 17. Computer workstation issues include all of the following except
a. visual difficulties.
b. muscular aches and pains.
c. job stress.
d. computer screens that are four to nine inches below eye level.

LO 4 _____ 18. Nutritional programs address lifestyle change in regards to
a. physical exercise.
b. a nutritional diet.
c. both of the above.
d. none of the above.

LO 4 _____ 19. At the present time, employee stress
a. is greater than it has been in years.
b. is useful in helping to boost productivity.
c. is about the same as it has always been.
d. has greatly improved.

LO 4 _____ 20. According to Duke University researchers, obese employees
a. have medical costs five times higher than non-obese workers.
b. miss eight times the number of workdays as non-obese workers.
c. cost companies an estimated 5.5 billion a year in lost productivity.
d. all of the above.

LO 5 _____ 21. A program referring employees in need of assistance to in-house counselors or outside professionals is a(n)
a. employee right-to-know program.
b. alarm reaction program.
c. employee assistance program.
d. voluntary protection program (VPP).

LO 5 _____ 22. When managers note that individual productivity is lowered, that morale problems exist, and that absenteeism and substance abuse are increasing, they are identifying the signs of
a. employee satisfaction.
b. employee depression.
c. union busting.
d. external environmental controls.

LO 5 _____ 23. Today one of the major employment issues affecting individuals is
    a. drug abuse.
    b. recycling of products.
    c. global warming.
    d. acid rain.

LO 5 _____ 24. Awakening the person to the reality of his or her situation is the first step in helping the
    a. individual through cultural shock.
    b. wellness committee.
    c. union organizing drive.
    d. alcoholic.

LO 5 _____ 25. Which act requires federal contractors and recipients of federal grants to take specific steps to ensure a drug-free work environment?
    a. The Drug-Free Workplace Act.
    b. Americans with Disabilities Act.
    c. Equal Pay Act.
    d. Fair Labor Standards Act.

LO 5 _____ 26. Physical activity and mental or emotional activity are two basic sources of
    a. job performance.
    b. employee turnover.
    c. chronic absenteeism.
    d. stress.

LO 5 _____ 27. Positive stress that accompanies achievement and exhilaration is
    a. distress.
    b. alarm reaction.
    c. eustress.
    d. job enrichment.

LO 5 _____ 28. Harmful stress characterized by a loss of feelings of security and adequacy is called
    a. distress.
    b. alarm reaction.
    c. eustress.
    d. job enrichment.

LO 5 _____ 29. High demand, high effort, low control, and low reward are identified as the primary factors in
   a. marital success.
   b. employee orientation.
   c. employee stress.
   d. employee training.

LO 5 _____ 30. The most severe stage of distress, manifesting itself in depression, frustration, and loss of productivity, is
   a. burnout.
   b. anxiety.
   c. nervousness.
   d. fatigue.

True/False

Identify the following statements as True or False.

Learning Outcome (LO)

LO 1 _____ 1. Improved productivity and wages and the lack of medical expenses coupled with decreased disabilities in the workplace led to the passage of the Occupational Safety and Health Act in 1970.

LO 1 _____ 2. OSHA cannot begin standards-setting procedures on its own initiative but instead must obtain approval from congress.

LO 1 _____ 3. Typically, the Occupational Safety and Health Act inspectors will arrive at a work site unannounced and ask for a meeting with a representative of the employer.

LO 1 _____ 4. The Occupational Safety and Health Act citations may be issued immediately following inspections or later by mail.

LO 1 _____ 5. Employees are not required to comply with all applicable Occupational Safety and Health Act standards, to report hazardous conditions, and to follow all employer safety and health rules and regulations, including those prescribing the use of protective equipment.

LO 1 _____ 6. The complaint most registered against the Occupational Safety and Health Administration is the even enforcement efforts by the agency from one political administration to the next.

LO 2 _____ 7. Typically HR or industrial relations is responsible for safety programs but the success of the programs depends on managers and supervisors.

163

LO 2 _____   8. One of a supervisor's major responsibilities is to communicate to employees the need to work safely.

LO 2 _____   9. Human resources professionals and safety directors do not encourage employee involvement when designing and implementing safety programs.

LO 2 _____   10. Penalties for violating safety rules are usually stated in the employee handbook.

LO 2 _____   11. The supervisor and a member of the safety committee do not need to investigate every accident.

LO 2 _____   12. The Occupational Safety and Health Act requirements mandate that employers with 11 or more employees maintain records of occupational injuries and illnesses.

LO 2 _____   13. An injury or illness is a recordable case if it results in death, days away from work, restricted work, transfer to another job, or medical treatment beyond first aid.

LO 3 _____   14. The Occupational Safety and Health Act is clearly designed to protect the health, as well as the safety, of employees.

LO 3 _____   15. Hazardous chemical containers do not have to be labeled with the identity of the contents but must state any appropriate hazard warnings.

LO 3 _____   16. When cumulative trauma disorders result from work activities, these injuries have been held by courts to be compensable injuries entailing workers' compensation payments.

LO 4 _____   17. It is recognized that better health not only benefits the individual but also pays off for the organization in reduced absenteeism, increased efficiency, better morale, and other savings.

LO 4 _____   18. Eustress is a form of stress that is positive.

LO 5 _____   19. Studies have shown that work-related stress contributes to injuries and illnesses.

LO 5 _____   20. The National Institute of Mental Health estimates that nearly 17 million Americans suffer from some form of physical impairment every year.

LO 5 _____   21. In confronting the problem, employers must recognize that alcoholism is a disease that follows a rather unpredictable course.

LO 5 _____   22. Alcoholism is regarded as a disease and is always treated as a physical impairment of the employee.

LO 5 _____   23. Stress becomes distress when a person begins to sense a loss of feelings of security and adequacy.

LO 5 _____   24. Career burnout, a severe stage of distress, generally occurs when a person begins questioning company values.

LO 5 _____   25. Under no circumstances should managers attempt to play amateur psychologist and attempt to diagnose an employee's condition.

Matching

Match each term with the proper definition.

Terms

a. burnout
b. cumulative trauma disorders
c. depression
d. distress
e. emergency action plan
f. eustress
g. fitness-for-duty evaluation
h. Material Safety Data Sheets (MSDSs)
i. recordable case
j. right-to-know laws
k. stress

Definitions

_____   1. injuries involving tendons of the fingers, hands, and arms that become inflamed from repeated stresses and strains.

_____   2. negative emotional state marked by feelings of low spirits, gloominess, sadness, and loss of pleasure in ordinary activities.

_____   3. harmful stress characterized by a loss of feelings of security and adequacy.

_____   4. The number of injuries and illnesses per 100 full-time employees during a given year.

_____   5. documents that contain vital information about hazardous substances.

_____   6. positive stress that accompanies achievement and exhilaration.

_____   7. any adjustive demand caused by physical, mental, or emotional factors that requires coping behavior.

_____ 8. laws that require employers to advise employees of job hazards.

_____ 9. most severe stage of distress, manifesting itself in depression, frustration, and loss of productivity.

_____ 10. any occupational death, illness, or injury to be recorded in the Occupational Safety and Health Act log.

Internet Exercises

What are the job factors that contribute to employee burnout?
http://stress.about.com/od/burnout/a/job_burnout.htm

What actions would you recommended to address workplace tragedy?
http://humanresources.about.com/od/healthsafetyandwellness/a/tragedy_work.htm

How to Inquire about a Safe and Healthy Work Environment

You are encouraged to inquire about a safe and healthy work environment with prospective employers. Safety is an important concern to everyone, and questions should be generated based on the philosophy of management and the firm's commitment to safety. Ask questions related to safety issues, such as the following: What are the major causes of accidents in the workplace? Does the Occupational Safety and Health Act regulate this work environment? Does the employer presently have a safety committee? What is its role and function? Is it a recommending body or does it have functional authority? Does the employer have a logbook to record accidents?

Health-related factors are important concerns for employees and should be addressed. Health hazards are those characteristics of the work environment that more slowly and systematically result in damage to the employee's health. Thus, health hazards impair working conditions and can result in decreased productivity and downtime. There are Occupational Safety and Health Act regulations pertaining to health requirements. You should address health-related issues, such as exposure to hazardous chemicals or toxic substances. Employers must disclose information to employees concerning any hazard that may pose an injury to their health. A smoking policy is becoming an important issue due to the increased hazard of second-hand smoke. For instance, smoking is prohibited in most state and federal offices. There are procedures and rules that may apply, and you are encouraged to become familiar with these regulations.

SOLUTIONS

Multiple Choice:	True/False:	Matching:

Multiple Choice:

1. c
2. b
3. a
4. d
5. b
6. d
7. b
8. a
9. b
10. c
11. d
12. d
13. b
14. c
15. b
16. b
17. d
18. c
19. a
20. d
21. c
22. b
23. a
24. d
25. a
26. d
27. c
28. a
29. c
30. a

True/False:

1. False
2. False
3. True
4. True
5. False
6. False
7. True
8. True
9. False
10. True
11. False
12. True
13. True
14. True
15. False
16. True
17. True
18. True
19. True
20. False
21. False
22. False
23. True
24. False
25. True

Matching:

1. c
2. d
3. e
4. a
5. h
6. g
7. j
8. f
9. b
10. i

False Statements Made True

1. **Lost** productivity and wages and **increasing** medical expenses coupled with **increased** disabilities in the workplace led to the passage of the Occupational Safety and Health Act in 1970.

2. OSHA **can** begin standards-setting procedures on its own initiative.

5. Employees **are** required to comply with all applicable Occupational Safety and Health Act standards, to report hazardous conditions, and to follow all employer safety and health rules and regulations, including those prescribing the use of protective equipment.

6. The complaint most registered against the Occupational Safety and Health Administration is the **uneven** enforcement efforts by the agency from one political administration to the next.

9. Human resources professionals and safety directors **advocate** employee involvement when designing and implementing safety programs.

11. The supervisor and a member of the safety committee **need** to investigate every accident.

15. Hazardous chemical containers **must** be labeled with the identity of the contents **and** must state any appropriate hazard warnings.

20. The National Institute of Mental Health estimates that nearly 17 million Americans suffer from **depression** every year.

21. In confronting the problem, employers must recognize that alcoholism is a disease that follows a rather **predictable** course.

22. Alcoholism is regarded as a disease **similar to a mental impairment** of the employee.

24. Career burnout, a severe stage of distress, generally occurs when a person begins questioning **his or her own personal** values.

CHAPTER 13

EMPLOYEE RIGHTS AND DISCIPLINE

The rights of employees to protect their jobs while obtaining fair and just treatment from employers received much attention during the 1990s. On the other side of the balance are the employer's responsibilities to provide a safe and efficient workplace for employees while expecting productivity and a positive attitude from all jobholders. Issues such as drug testing, smoking on the job, access to one's personnel file, notice of plant closing, and unfair discharge are therefore topics of interest to all organizational members.

When employees exhibit unsatisfactory behavior or performance, it may be necessary for an employer to take disciplinary action against them. If the employee is represented by a union, the disciplinary action is likely to be appealed through the grievance procedure provided for in the labor agreement. In a nonunion organization, the aggrieved employee may use an alternative dispute-resolution procedure established specifically by the employer. In either the union or nonunion setting, management may ultimately have to defend its position to a specified individual or group who will decide on the reasonableness of the action taken. To defend themselves successfully, as well as to simply impose fair and objective disciplinary procedures, supervisors and managers need to understand the principles of effective discipline.

Organizational ethics extends beyond the legal requirements of managing employees in human resources management. Managers must comply with governmental regulations to promote an environment free from litigation. However, beyond what is required by law are the matters of organizational ethics and the ethical or unethical behavior engaged in by managers.

LEARNING OUTCOMES

After studying this chapter, you should be able to

LEARNING OUTCOME 1   Explain the concepts of employee rights and employer responsibilities.

LEARNING OUTCOME 2
Explain the concepts of employment-at-will, wrongful discharge, implied contract, and constructive discharge.

LEARNING OUTCOME 3
Identify and explain what the privacy rights of employees are.

LEARNING OUTCOME 4
Discuss the meaning of discipline and why managers cannot ignore disciplinary problems.

LEARNING OUTCOME 5
Explain how to establish disciplinary policies and investigate disciplinary problems.

LEARNING OUTCOME 6
Differentiate between the two approaches to disciplinary action.

LEARNING OUTCOME 7
Identify the different types of alternative dispute resolution methods.

LEARNING OUTCOME 8
Discuss the role of ethics in the management of human resources.

CHAPTER SUMMARY RELATING TO LEARNING OUTCOMES

LEARNING OUTCOME   Workers have certain expectations about the employment relationship they have with their employers, including the mutual obligations they have to one another. Included among those expectations are a certain degree of privacy and fair and equitable treatment while on the job. Employers, however, have the responsibility to monitor the activities of their workers in order to provide a safe and secure workplace free from harmful employee acts. When the perceived rights of employees differ from the reasonable responsibilities of management, conflict can result.

LEARNING OUTCOME 2   The employment-at-will doctrine gives employees and employers the right to terminate their employment relationship with one another at any time; the implied contract concept is an exception to the employment-at-will doctrine. Under this concept, an employer's oral or written statements may constitute a contractual obligation in which case the at-will doctrine does not apply. Constructive discharge occurs when an employee voluntarily terminates employment but subsequently alleges that he or she was forced to quit because of intolerable working conditions imposed by the employer. Employees may claim they are retaliated against when employers punish them for exercising their rights under law or for receiving favorable EEOC or court awards.

LEARNING OUTCOME 3   Once employed, employees expect certain privacy rights such as freedom from unwarranted intrusion into their personal affairs. Laws and court cases related to workplace privacy generally attempt to balance employees' legitimate expectation of privacy against the need of employers to supervise and control the efficient operations of the organizations. Testing for substance abuse and searching and monitoring employees while on the job and off are among the many privacy-rights issues employers and their workers face.

LEARNING OUTCOME 4   In the context of management, discipline does not mean punishment. Rather, discipline is a tool used to correct the practices of employees to help them perform better so they conform to acceptable standards. Even when it is justified, managers do not generally enjoy disciplining their employees. However, failing to do so generally aggravates a problem that eventually must be resolved.

LEARNING OUTCOME 5   A firm's HR professionals, in combination with other managers, should establish disciplinary policies, or rules, that relate to the safe and efficient operation of the organization. The rules should be written down, explained, widely communicated within the organization, and consistently applied. They should also be revised regularly as laws, regulations, and court rulings change. An investigation of an infraction begins with properly documenting it. To determine the severity of the disciplinary measure, managers need to know whether the employee knew of the rule that was violated, any extenuating circumstances that might justify the employee's conduct, the employee's past work record, and various other factors.

LEARNING OUTCOME 6   The two approaches to discipline are progressive discipline and positive discipline. Progressive discipline follows a series of steps based on increasing the degrees of corrective action. Positive discipline, based upon reminders, is a cooperative discipline approach in which employees accept responsibility for the desired employee improvement. The corrective action taken should match the severity of the misconduct.

LEARNING OUTCOME 7   Alternative dispute resolution procedures are ways to resolve disputes out of court while ensuring employees receive fair treatment. The most common forms of ADRs are step-review systems, peer-review systems, the open-door system, the ombudsman system, mediation, and arbitration.

LEARNING OUTCOME   Ethics in HRM extends beyond the legal requirements of managing employees. Managers engage in ethical behavior when employees are treated in an objective and fair way and when an employee's personal and work-related rights are respected and valued.

REVIEW QUESTIONS

Multiple Choice

Choose the letter of the word or phrase that best completes each statement.

Learning Outcome (LO)

LO 1 _____ 1. The guarantee of fair treatment that employees expect in protection of their employment status is
    a. employee rights.
    b. equal pay for equal work.
    c. fair employment.
    d. performance appraisal.

LO 1 _____ 2. The failure to provide a reasonable amount of care where such failure results in injury to another person is
    a. punishment.
    b. suspension.
    c. negligence.
    d. severance pay.

LO 2 _____ 3. When an employee agrees to work for an employer for an unspecified period, the resulting relationship is called
    a. alternative dispute resolution.
    b. business ethics.
    c. employment-at-will.
    d. negligence.

LO 2 _____ 4. In *Adair v. United States* the Supreme Court upheld
    a. alternative dispute resolution programs.
    b. the need for ethical behavior in firms.
    c. employment-at-will doctrine.
    d. negligence doctrine.

LO 2 _____ 5. Which agency administers the whistle-blowing provisions in 15 federal statutes?
    a. EEOC.
    b. OSHA.
    c. NLRB.
    d. FCC.

LO 2 _____   6. Agreements that prohibit ex-employees from soliciting clients or customers of former employers for a specified period of time are called
   a. non-compete agreements.
   b. intellectual property agreement.
   c. non-piracy agreements.
   d. employment-at-will agreements.

LO 2 _____   7. Oral or written statements made during the preemployment process or subsequent to hiring are
   a. employment-at-will contracts.
   b. employee rights.
   c. business ethics.
   d. implied contractual rights.

LO 2 _____   8. An employee's voluntary termination of his or her employment because of harsh, unreasonable employment conditions placed upon the individual by the employer is called
   a. employee assistance.
   b. constructive discharge.
   c. human resources planning.
   d. job evaluation.

LO 2 _____   9. WARN Act requires organizations with more than 100 employees to give employees and their communities how many days notice of any closure or layoff affecting 50 or more full-time employees?
   a. 50 days.
   b. 60 days.
   c. 70 days.
   d. 80 days.

LO 3 _____   10. Personal freedom from unwarranted government or business intrusion into personal affairs involves
   a. due process.
   b. job expectancy rights.
   c. rights of privacy.
   d. performance evaluation.

LO 3 _____   11. Substance abusers
   a. are five times more likely to file workers' comp claims.
   b. are 33 percent less productive.
   c. use 16 times as many health care benefits.
   d. do all of the above.

LO 3 _____ 12. Unless state or local laws either restrict or prohibit drug testing, in case of probable cause, private employers have a right to require employees to submit to a
    a. polygraph test.
    b. lie detector test.
    c. psychiatric evaluation.
    d. urinalysis or blood test.

LO 3 _____ 13. It is not uncommon for employers to monitor the behavior of individual conduct in the workplace through
    a. job evaluation.
    b. job analysis.
    c. equal pay for equal work.
    d. surveillance techniques.

LO 3 _____ 14. Impairment testing involves all of the following except
    a. it is also called fitness for duty.
    b. serving a means of testing HR tests to see if they are impaired.
    c. measures whether an employee is sufficiently alert.
    d. identifies problems a drug test cannot.

LO 4 _____ 15. Discipline involves
    a. punishment.
    b. vengeance.
    c. correction.
    d. none of the above.

LO 4 _____ 16. The primary responsibility for preventing or correcting disciplinary problems is
    a. the immediate supervisor.
    b. the HR manager.
    c. the CEO.
    d. the board of directors.

LO 4 _____ 17. Failing to discipline employees when appropriate
    a. demotivates an organization.
    b. makes later disciplinary action more difficult.
    c. raises questions about any satisfactory ratings or merit pay given when discipline finally occurs..
    d. all of the above.

LO 5 _____   18. Questions to consider during disciplinary investigations include all of the
following except
a. did the employee know that he or she was doing something wrong?
b. will discipline destroy the friendship?
c. are there extenuating circumstances?
d. has the rule been uniformly enforced?

LO 5 _____   19. A manager's record of employee misconduct
a. is considered a business document.
b. is admissible evidence is courts of law.
c. both of the above.
d. none of the above.

LO 6 _____   20. If a thorough investigation shows that an employee has violated an
organization rule, the supervisor should impose
a. due process.
b. oral warnings.
c. compensatory damages.
d. disciplinary action.

LO 6 _____   21. The two primary approaches to disciplinary action are
a. progressive and positive discipline.
b. peer reviews and open-door policies.
c. outplacement and ombudsman services.
d. employment-at-will and implied contracts.

LO 6 _____   22. An application of corrective measures by increasing degrees designed to
motivate an employee to correct his or her misconduct voluntarily is
a. constructive discharge.
b. due process.
c. progressive discipline.
d. negative discipline.

LO 6 _____   23. The approach that focuses on the early correction of misconduct, with
the employee taking total responsibility for resolving the problem, is
a. orientation and training.
b. job security.
c. positive discipline.
d. merit review.

LO 6 _____   24. When employees fail to conform to organizational rules and regulations,
the final disciplinary action in many cases is a
a. peer review.
b. discharge.
c. verbal warning.
d. written reprimand.

LO 6 _____ 25. An employee's right to present his or her position during a disciplinary action is
    a. employment-at-will.
    b. due process.
    c. implied contract.
    d. willful discharge.

LO 7 _____ 26. The term used to describe the different types of employee complaint resolution procedures is
    a. discipline.
    b. employment-at-will principle.
    c. business ethics.
    d. alternative dispute resolution.

LO 7 _____ 27. Listening to an employee's complaint and attempting to resolve it by mediating a solution between the employee and the supervisor is the function of a(n)
    a. shop steward.
    b. corporate executive.
    c. ombudsman.
    d. stockholder.

LO 7 _____ 28. The process that is used primarily to resolve discrimination suits by private employers in areas of age, gender, sexual harassment, and race is
    a. job evaluation.
    b. arbitration.
    c. mediation.
    d. conciliation.

LO 8 _____ 29. What can be defined as a set of standards of acceptable conduct and moral judgment?
    a. social responsibility.
    b. ethics
    c. human resources planning.
    d. job enlargement.

LO 8 _____ 30. The ultimate goal of ethics training is to
    a. create social responsibility.
    b. treat employees in a fair and equitable manner.
    c. implement human resources planning.
    d. facilitate job enlargement.

True/False

Identify the following statements as True or False.

Learning Outcome(LO)

LO 1 _____   1. The U.S. Constitution guarantees that jobs are among the specific property rights of employers.

LO 2 _____   2. The principle of employment-at-will assumes employers are free to terminate the employment relationship at any time, and without notice, for any reason, no reason, or even a bad reason.

LO 2 _____   3. The significance of wrongful discharge suits is that they challenge the employer's right under the implied employment concept to bilaterally discharge employees.

LO 3 _____   4. Drug testing is most prevalent among employees in sensitive positions within the public sector, in organizations doing business with the federal government, and in public and private transportation outfits.

LO 3 _____   5. Employers subject to the Americans with Disabilities Act need not comply with the law's provisions regarding drug addiction.

LO 3 _____   6. Employees have limited expectation of privacy in places where work rules that provide for inspections have been put into effect; they do not have to comply with probable-cause searches by employers.

LO 3 _____   7. The information kept in an employee's personnel file does not have a significant impact, positive or negative, on career development.

LO 3 _____   8. The right to privacy does not extend to email and voice mail messages.

LO 4 _____   9. A major responsibility of the human resources department is to develop and to have top management approve its disciplinary policies and procedures.

LO 5 _____   10. Setting an organization's rules is the foundation for an effective disciplinary system.

LO 5 _____   11. A major reason for the reversal of disciplinary actions is the failure to communicate rules.

LO 5 _____ 12. One question to consider during disciplinary investigations is "What are the facts?"

LO 5 _____ 13. The most significant cause of inadequate documentation is that managers often do not know what constitutes good documentation.

LO 6 _____ 14. The sequence and severity of the disciplinary action vary with the type of offense and the circumstances surrounding it.

LO 6 _____ 15. While positive discipline appears similar to progressive discipline, its emphasis is on giving employees reprimands rather than reminders as a way to improve performance.

LO 6 _____ 16. The right of the employee to tell his or her side of the story regarding the alleged infraction of organizational rules is an employee assistance program.

LO 7 _____ 17. A procedure that allows the employee to submit a complaint to successively higher levels of management is the step-review system.

LO 7 _____ 18. The peer-review system can be used as the sole method for resolving employee complaints or it can be used in conjunction with a step-review system.

LO 7 _____ 19. Two of the major weaknesses of an open-door policy are the willingness of managers to listen honestly to employees and the willingness of workers to approach managers with their complaints.

LO 7 _____ 20. Since the ombudsman has no authority to finalize a solution to the problem, compromises are highly possible and all concerned tend to feel satisfied with the outcome.

LO 7 _____ 21. Mediation employs a neutral third party to assist employees and managers to reach a voluntary agreement unacceptable to both parties.

LO 7 _____ 22. Arbitration agreements may prevent employees from suing their employer in court, and may preclude employees from filing discrimination charges with the Equal Employment Opportunity Commission.

LO 8 _____ 23. Managers need not comply with governmental regulation to promote an environment free from litigation.

LO 8 _____   24. Compliance with laws and the behavioral treatment of employees are two completely different aspects of the manager's job.

LO 8 _____   25. Many organizations have their own code of ethics that governs relations with employees and the public at large.

Matching

Match each term with the proper definition.

Terms

a.	alternative dispute resolution (ADR)	k.	ombudsman
b.	constructive discharge	l.	open-door policy
c.	discipline	m.	peer-review system
d.	due process	n.	positive, or nonpunitive, discipline
e.	employee rights	o.	progressive discipline
f.	employment-at-will principle	p.	psychological contract
g.	ethics	q.	step-review system
h.	impairment testing	r.	whistle-blowing
i.	mediation	s.	wrongful discharge
j.	negligence		

Definitions

_____   1. application of corrective measures by increasing stages.

_____   2. system for reviewing employee complaints that utilizes a group composed of equal numbers of employee representatives and management appointees, which functions as a jury since its members weigh evidence, consider arguments, and, after deliberation, vote independently to render a final decision.

_____   3. failure to provide reasonable care where such failure results in injury to consumers or other employees.

_____   4. technique applied to different types of employee complaint or dispute-resolution procedures.

_____   5. the use of an impartial neutral party to reach a compromise decision in employment disputes.

_____ 6. employee's right to present his or her position during a disciplinary action.

_____ 7. system of discipline that focuses on the early correction of employee misconduct, with the employee taking total responsibility for correcting the problem.

_____ 8. policy of settling grievances that identifies various levels of management above the immediate supervisor for employee contact.

_____ 9. the right of an employer to fire an employee without giving a reason and the right of an employee to quit when he or she chooses.

_____ 10. system for reviewing employee complaints and disputes by successively higher levels of management.

_____ 11. definitions include (1) treatment that punishes; (2) orderly behavior in an organizational setting; or (3) training that molds and strengthens desirable conduct or corrects undesirable conduct and develops self-control.

_____ 12. designated individual from whom employees may seek counsel for the resolution of their complaints.

_____ 13. guarantees of fair treatment from employers, particularly regarding an employee's right to privacy.

_____ 14. measures whether an employee is alert enough to work. Also call fitness-for-duty or performance-based testing.

_____ 15. set of standards of conduct and moral judgments that help to determine right and wrong behavior.

_____ 16. an employee voluntarily terminating his or her employment because of harsh, unreasonable employment conditions placed upon the individual by the employer.

_____ 17. expectations of a fair exchange of employment obligations between an employee and employer.

_____ 18. complaints to governmental agencies by employees about their employers' illegal or immoral acts or practices.

_____ 19. a discharge, or termination, of an employee that is illegal

Internet Exercises

When can constructive discharge be upheld?
http://www.legalworkplace.com/termination/constructive-discharge.aspx

What is an employee bill of rights?
http://www.findarticles.com/p/articles/mi_m0MNT/is_4_57/ai_99932979.

How to Develop and Utilize Ethical Codes in the Business World

Ethical codes are extremely relevant especially when working in an organization that is customer driven. For example, IBM's mission is to be customer-driven to create consumer satisfaction at all costs. When joining an organization, you must have orientation and training on ethical codes, policies, and procedures.

Ethics can be defined as a set of standards of acceptable conduct and moral judgment. Ethics provides cultural guidelines, organizational or societal, that help decide between proper and improper conduct. Ethics in human resources management extends beyond the legal requirements of managing employees. Managers engage in ethical behavior when employees are treated in an objective and fair way and when an employee's personal and work-related rights are respected and valued.

Organizations have ethics committees to provide training to employees. The ultimate goals of ethics training are to avoid unethical behavior and adverse publicity and to gain a strategic advantage but most of all, to treat employees in a fair and equitable manner, recognizing them as productive members of the organization.

SOLUTIONS

Multiple Choice:	True/False:	Matching:
1. a	1. False	1. o
2. c	2. True	2. m
3. c	3. False	3. j
4. c	4. True	4. a
5. b	5. False	5. i
6. c	6. False	6. d
7. d	7. False	7. n
8. b	8. True	8. l
9. b	9. True	9. f
10. c	10. True	10. q
11. d	11. True	11. c
12. d	12. True	12. k
13. d	13. True	13. e
14. b	14. True	14. h
15. c	15. False	15. g
16. a	16. False	16. b
17. d	17. True	17. p
18. b	18. True	18. r
19. c	19. False	19. s
20. d	20. True	
21. a	21. False	
22. c	22. False	
23. c	23. False	
24. b	24. True	
25. b	25. True	
26. d		
27. c		
28. b		
29. b		
30. b		

False Statements Made True

1. The U.S. Constitution **carries no mandate that** guarantees that jobs are among the specific property rights of employers.

3. The significance of wrongful discharge suits is that they challenge the employer's right under the **employment-at-will** concept to bilaterally discharge employees.

5. Employers subject to the Americans with Disabilities Act **must** comply with the law's provisions regarding drug addiction.

6. Employees have limited **reasonable** expectation of privacy in places where work rules that provide for inspections have been put into effect; they **must** comply with probable-cause searches by employers.

7. The information kept in an employee's personnel file **can** have a significant impact, positive or negative, on career development.

15. While positive discipline appears similar to progressive discipline, its emphasis is on giving employees **reminders** rather than **reprimands** as a way to improve performance.

16. The right of the employee to tell his or her side of the story regarding the alleged infraction of organizational rules is **due process**.

19. Two of the major weaknesses of an open-door policy are the **unwillingness** of managers to listen honestly to employees and the **reluctance** of workers to approach managers with their complaints.

21. Mediation employs a neutral third party to assist employees and managers to reach a voluntary agreement **acceptable** to both parties.

22. Arbitration agreements may prevent employees from suing their employer in court; **they cannot** preclude employees from filing discrimination charges with the Equal Employment Opportunity Commission.

23. Managers **must** comply with governmental regulation to promote an environment free from litigation.

CHAPTER 14

THE DYNAMICS OF LABOR RELATIONS

Workers unionize so they can influence employer decisions affecting their employment conditions and general welfare. When employees are unionized, human resources policies can no longer be determined unilaterally by the employer. Instead, these policies and practices are subject to the terms of the labor agreement that has been negotiated with the union. A major responsibility of the local union officers is to ensure that these terms are observed and that the rights of members provided by the agreement are protected. Labor agreements, which determine conditions of employment for union members, are achieved through collective bargaining. Bargaining success depends not only on the skills of the negotiators but also on the power each side can exercise to support its bargaining demands. Once the contract is ratified, its terms and conditions of employment bind both parties until it is renegotiated. During the period the contract is in force, the parties learn to cooperate through the administration of the agreement. When conflict arises over the rights the contract grants to each side, the grievance/arbitration provisions of the contract are invoked to resolve these differences.

LEARNING OUTCOMES

After studying this chapter, you should be able to

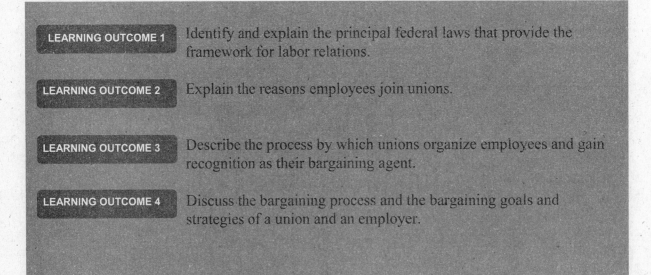

LEARNING OUTCOME 1   Identify and explain the principal federal laws that provide the framework for labor relations.

LEARNING OUTCOME 2   Explain the reasons employees join unions.

LEARNING OUTCOME 3   Describe the process by which unions organize employees and gain recognition as their bargaining agent.

LEARNING OUTCOME 4   Discuss the bargaining process and the bargaining goals and strategies of a union and an employer.

LEARNING OUTCOME 5	Differentiate the forms of bargaining power that a union and an employer may utilize to enforce their bargaining demands.
LEARNING OUTCOME 6	Describe a typical union grievance procedure and explain the basis for arbitration awards.
LEARNING OUTCOME 7	Discuss some of the contemporary challenges to labor organizations.

CHAPTER SUMMARY RELATING TO LEARNING OUTCOMES

LEARNING OUTCOME 1   The Railway Labor Act (1926) affords collective bargaining rights to workers employed in the railway and airline industries. The Norris-LaGuardia Act (1932) imposes limitations on the granting of injunctions in labor-management disputes. Most private employees are granted representation rights through the Wagner Act (1935), which has helped protect and encourage union organizing and bargaining activities. The passage of the Taft-Hartley Act (1947) and the Landrum-Griffin Act (1959) has served to establish certain controls over the internal affairs of unions and their relations with employers.

LEARNING OUTCOME 2   Studies show that workers unionize for different economic, psychological, and social reasons. While some employees may join unions because they are required to do so, most belong to unions because they are convinced that unions help them to improve their wages, benefits, and most importantly, equality. Employee unionization is largely caused by dissatisfaction with managerial practices and procedures.

LEARNING OUTCOME 3   A formal union organizing campaign is used to solicit employee support for the union. Once employees demonstrate their desire to unionize through signing authorization cards, the union petitions the National Labor Relations Board (NLRB) for a secret-ballot election. If 51 percent of those voting in the election vote for the union, the NLRB certifies the union as the bargaining representative for all employees in the bargaining unit.

LEARNING OUTCOME 4   Negotiating a labor agreement is a detailed process. Each side prepares a list of proposals it wishes to achieve while additionally trying to anticipate proposals desired by the other side. Bargaining teams must be selected and all proposals must be analyzed to determine their impact on and cost to the organization. Both employer and union negotiators are sensitive to current bargaining patterns within the industry, general cost-of-living trends, and geographical wage differentials. Managers establish goals that seek to retain control over operations and to minimize costs. Union negotiators focus their demands around improved wages, hours, and working conditions. An agreement is reached when both sides compromise their original positions and final terms fall within the limits of the parties' bargaining zone.

Traditionally, collective bargaining between labor and management has been adversarial. Presently, there is an increased interest in non-adversarial negotiations—negotiations based on mutual gains and a heightened respect between the parties. What the FMCS calls interest-based bargaining is one form of non-adversarial negotiations.

LEARNING OUTCOME 5 The collective bargaining process includes not only the actual negotiations, but also the power tactics used to support negotiating demands. When negotiations become deadlocked, bargaining becomes a power struggle to force from either side the concessions needed to break the deadlock. The union's power in collective bargaining comes from its ability to picket, strike, or boycott the employer. The employer's power during negotiations comes from its ability to lock out employees or to operate during a strike by using managerial or replacement employees.

LEARNING OUTCOME 6 When differences arise between labor and management, they are normally resolved through the grievance procedure. Grievance procedures are negotiated and thus reflect the needs and desires of the parties. The typical grievance procedure will consist of three, four, or five steps— each step having specific filing and reply times. Higher-level managers and union officials become involved in disputes at the higher steps of the grievance procedure. The final step of the grievance procedure may be arbitration. Arbitrators render a final decision to problems not resolved at lower grievance steps.

The submission agreement is a statement of the issue to be solved through arbitration. It is simply the problem the parties wish to have settled. The arbitrator must answer the issue by basing the arbitration award on four factors: contents of the labor agreement (or employment policy), submission agreement as written, testimony and evidence obtained at the hearing, and various arbitration standards developed over time to assist in the resolution of different types of labor-management disputes. Arbitration is not an exact science because arbitrators give varying degrees of importance to the evidence and criteria by which disputes are resolved.

LEARNING OUTCOME 7 Challenges facing union leaders today include declining membership caused by technological advancements and increased domestic and global competition. Offshoring is when jobs done in one country are lost to another country. Companies argue that to remain competitive they must offshore more and more jobs to lower wage economies. While technological change has much more to do with job loss in America, employers need to be more open in their decisions to move jobs offshore or to replace them with technology.

REVIEW QUESTIONS

Multiple Choice

Choose the letter of the word or phrase that best completes each statement.

Learning Outcome (LO)

LO 1 _____   1. The act that severely restricted the ability of employers to obtain an injunction forbidding a union from engaging in peaceful picketing, boycotts, or various striking activities is the
   a. Taft-Hartley Act.
   b. Wagner Act.
   c. Norris-LaGuardia Act.
   d. Landrum-Griffin Act.

LO 1 _____   2. The agency responsible for administering and enforcing the Wagner Act is the
   a. Affirmative Action Committee.
   b. Equal Employment Opportunity Commission.
   c. Occupational Safety and Health Administration.
   d. National Labor Relations Board.

LO 1 _____   3. Union self-organizing activities and collective bargaining were legalized through the
   a. Wagner Act.
   b. Taft-Hartley Act.
   c. Norris-LaGuardia Act.
   d. Landrum-Griffin Act.

LO 1 _____   4. Section 8 of which act lists unfair labor practices of employers?
   a. Wagner Act.
   b. Taft-Hartley Act.
   c. Norris-LaGuardia Act.
   d. Landrum-Griffin Act.

LO 1 _____   5. Which act lists unfair labor practices of unions?
   a. Wagner Act.
   b. Taft-Hartley Act.
   c. Norris-LaGuardia Act.
   d. Landrum-Griffin Act.

LO 1 _____   6. The Landrum-Griffin Act of 1959 states that every union member has been given the following rights, *except*
   a. nominating candidates for union office.
   b. voting in union elections or referendums.
   c. attending union meetings.
   d. creating featherbedding.

LO 2 _____   7. A provision of the labor agreement that requires employees to join the union as a requirement for their employment is called
   a. management prerogatives.
   b. closed ship.
   c. agency shop.
   d. union shop.

LO 2 _____   8. The strongest reasons to join a labor union are the traditional issues of dissatisfaction with wages, benefits, and
   a. management prerogatives.
   b. working conditions.
   c. compulsory arbitration.
   d. job design.

LO 2 _____   9. When employees perceive that managerial practices regarding promotion, transfer, shift assignment, or other job-related policies are administered in an unfair or biased manner, they may seek
   a. decertification.
   b. mediation.
   c. unionization.
   d. binding arbitration.

LO 2 _____   10. The major concerns for which employees join unions involve
   a. social and leadership needs.
   b. esteem and self-actualization.
   c. job enlargement and enrichment.
   d. achievement and physiological requirements.

LO 3 _____   11. Unions have been shocked into more aggressive and creative tactics in organizing strategies to counteract employer antiunion campaigns and to compensate for a(n)
   a. closed-shop agreement.
   b. decline in membership.
   c. organizational picketing event.
   d. wildcat strike.

LO 3 _____ 12. Once the union is certified, the employer is obligated to begin negotiations leading toward a(n)
   a. grievance.
   b. wildcat strike.
   c. authorization card.
   d. labor agreement.

LO 3 _____ 13. What percentage of employees within a bargaining unit must a union succeed in signing up, before thay can petition for an NLRB conducted election?
   a. 30%.
   b. 40%.
   c. 50%.
   d. 60%.

LO 3 _____ 14. Unions seek greater participation in management decisions that involve such issues as subcontracting of work, productivity standards, and job content as a result of
   a. job security.
   b. management prerogatives.
   c. working conditions.
   d. hours of work.

LO 3 _____ 15. In 2005, six unions split from the AFL-CIO to form
   a. American Federation of Teachers.
   b. AFSCME.
   c. Change to Win.
   d. National Education Association.

LO 3 _____ 16. To the "rank-and-file" union member, the importance of unionism resides in the activities of the
   a. piece-rate systems.
   b. management.
   c. self-managed teams.
   d. local union and its leaders.

LO 4 _____ 17. In collective bargaining there are economic pressures in the form of lockouts, plant closures, and the replacement of strikers that are used by the
   a. business agent.
   b. labor union.
   c. employer.
   d. shop steward.

LO 4 _____ 18. In collective bargaining, all matters concerning rates of pay, wages, hours of employment, or other conditions of employment are examples of
    a. mandatory subjects.
    b. voluntary issues.
    c. illegal subjects.
    d. unauthorized subjects.

LO 4 _____ 19. Areas or subjects where management and labor are free to bargain but neither side can force the other side to bargain are
    a. mandatory subjects.
    b. involuntary issues.
    c. illegal subjects.
    d. permissive issues.

LO 4 _____ 20. Illegal subjects in collective bargaining would include the closed-shop security agreement and
    a. wages and salaries.
    b. compulsory dues check-off.
    c. working conditions.
    d. hours of work.

LO 4 _____ 21. The area within which the union and the employer are willing to concede when negotiating is called the
    a. bargaining zone.
    b. impasse zone.
    c. management lockout.
    d. wildcat strike.

LO 5 _____ 22. The refusal of a group of employees to perform their jobs and withhold their services when negotiations become deadlocked is a
    a. lockout.
    b. boycott.
    c. strike.
    d. grievance procedure.

LO 5 _____ 23. When a union asks its members or customers not to patronize a business where there is a labor dispute, it is asking for a
    a. labor strike.
    b. company lockout.
    c. slowdown.
    d. boycott.

LO 5 _____ 24. Right-to-work laws ban
  a. labor strike.
  b. company lockout.
  c. slowdown.
  d. any form of compulsory union membership.

LO 5 _____ 25. A third party that can be utilized to recommend a compromise when the disputing parties are unable to resolve their differences is called a
  a. mediator.
  b. negotiator.
  c. business agent.
  d. narrator.

LO 5 _____ 26. An individual who has binding authority to resolve disputes arising in connection with the administration of an agreement is a(n)
  a. mediator.
  b. arbitrator.
  c. business agent.
  d. human resources director.

LO 5 _____ 27. In the public sector, where strikes are largely prohibited, a common method used in the attempt to resolve bargaining deadlocks is
  a. conciliation.
  b. interest arbitration.
  c. outsourcing.
  d. performance appraisal.

LO 6 _____ 28. Considered by some authorities to be the heart of the bargaining agreement, the safety valve that gives flexibility to the whole system of collective bargaining is the
  a. arbitration panel.
  b. primary boycott.
  c. grievance procedure.
  d. closed-shop security provision.

LO 6 _____ 29. Unions have a legal obligation to provide assistance to members who are pursuing a grievance under the
  a   secondary boycott award.
  b. employment-at-will doctrine.
  c. closed-shop security provision.
  d. fair representation doctrine.

LO 7 _____ 30. The fastest-growing segment of working people as potent prospects for union growth are
    a. professional employees.
    b. craft employees.
    c. self-managed teams.
    d. immigrants.

True/False

Identify the following statements as True or False.

LO 1 _____ 1. The primary purpose of the Railway Labor Act is to create the use of injunctions between labor and management.

LO 1 _____ 2. Before an injunction may be issued, employers need not show that lack of an injunction will cause greater harm to the employer than to the union.

LO 1 _____ 3. The Wagner Act created the National Labor Relations Board to govern labor relations in the United States.

LO 1 _____ 4. Because of the high incidence of strikes after World War II, the Taft-Hartley Act created the Federal Mediation and Conciliation Service to help resolve negotiating disputes.

LO 3 _____ 5. Most labor-organizing campaigns are undertaken by union organizers rather than employees.

LO 3 _____ 6. At least 30 percent of the employees must sign authorization cards before the National Labor Relations Board will hold a representation election.

LO 3 _____ 7. After the election is held, the winning party will be determined on the basis of the number of members of the bargaining unit.

LO 3 _____ 8. The petition to hold representation elections is always initiated by the employer.

LO 3 _____ 9. The center of power in the labor movement resides with national and international unions.

LO 3 _____   10. Depending on the size of the local union, one or more officers, in addition to the business representative, may be paid by the union to serve on a full-time basis.

LO 3 _____   11. Union stewards are normally elected by union members within their department and are always paid a union salary.

LO 3 _____   12. Business unionism (the general label given to the goals of American labor organizations) involves increased pay and benefits, job security, and improved working conditions.

LO 3 _____   13. Most state legislatures have granted public employees the right to strike.

LO 4 _____   14. Negotiators for an employer should develop a written plan called a proposal, which includes the collective bargaining strategy.

LO 4 _____   15. The initial meeting of the bargaining teams is a particularly important one because it establishes the climate that will prevail during the negotiations that follow.

LO 4 _____   16. Once bargaining begins, an employer is not obligated to negotiate in good faith with the union's representative over conditions of employment.

LO 5 _____   17. When negotiations become deadlocked, the employer's bargaining power largely rests on being able to continue operations in the face of a strike or to shut down operations entirely.

LO 5 _____   18. If employees decide to strike the organization, employers have the right to hire replacement workers.

LO 5 _____   19. A mediator assumes the role of a decision maker and determines what the settlement between the two parties should be.

LO 6 _____   20. If a grievance cannot be resolved through the grievance procedure, each disputing party must decide whether to use arbitration to resolve the case.

LO 6 _____   21. A grievance should be viewed as something to be won or lost from the perspective of the government.

LO 6 _____ 22. The arbitration hearing process begins with the swearing-in of witnesses and the introduction of the submission agreement, which is a statement of the problem to be resolved.

LO 6 _____ 23. The arbitration award should include not only the arbitrator's decision but also the rationale for it.

LO 6 _____ 24. Arbitrators are essentially constrained to decide cases based on the wording of the labor agreement but never to the facts, testimony, and evidence presented at the hearing.

LO 7 _____ 25. Targeted prospects for union growth include low-wage service workers on the bottom tier of the U.S. economy and recent immigrants who are working.

Matching

Match each term with the proper definition.

Terms

a. arbitrator
b. authorization card
c. bargaining power
d. bargaining unit
e. bargaining zone
f. business unionism
g. collective bargaining process
h. craft unions
i. employee associations

j. exclusive representation
k. fair representation doctrine
l. grievance procedure
m. industrial unions
n. interest-based bargaining
o. labor relations process
p. rights arbitration
q. unfair labor practices (ULPs)
r. union shop
s. union steward
t. offshoring

Definitions

_____ 1. specific employer and union illegal practices that operate to deny employees their rights and benefits under federal labor law.

_____ 2. unions that represent skilled craft workers.

_____ 3. a statement signed by an employee authorizing a union to act as a representative of the employee for purposes of collective bargaining.

_____   4. employee who as a non-paid union official represents the interests of members in their relations with management.

_____   5. logical sequence of four events: (1) workers desire collective representation, (2) union begins its organizing campaign, (3) collective negotiations lead to a contract, and (4) the contract is administered.

_____   6. term applied to the goals of U.S. labor organizations, which collectively bargain for improvements in wages, hours, job security, and working conditions.

_____   7. labor organizations that represent various groups of professional and white-collar employees in labor-management relations.

_____   8. provision of the labor agreement that requires employees to join the union as a condition of their employment.

_____   9. unions that represent all workers—skilled, semiskilled, unskilled—employed along industry lines.

_____   10. group of two or more employees who share common employment interests and conditions and may reasonably be grouped together for purposes of collective bargaining.

_____   11. formal procedure that provides for the union to represent members and nonmembers in processing a grievance.

_____   12. doctrine under which unions have a legal obligation to provide assistance to both members and nonmembers in labor relations matters.

_____   13. arbitration over interpretation of the meaning of contract terms or employee work grievances.

_____   14. process of negotiating a labor agreement, including the use of economic pressures by both parties.

_____   15. neutral third party who resolves a labor dispute by issuing a final decision in the disagreement.

_____   16. problem-solving bargaining based on a win-win philosophy and the development of a positive long-term relationship.

_____   17. the power of labor and management to achieve their goals through economic, social, or political influence.

_____ 18. the legal right and responsibility of the union to represent all bargaining unit members equally regardless of whether employees join the union or not.

_____ 19. area within which the union and the employer are willing to concede when bargaining.

_____ 20. work that was previously carried out in one country to another.

Internet Exercise

How can the arbitration process be expedited?
http://www.findarticles.com/p/articles/mi_qa3923/is_200305/ai_n9282717.

How to Manage a Nonunion Operation

Managing a nonunion operation is paramount for the success of an organization. Management must create an environment of openness, trust, and respect for the firm's employees. Managers must demonstrate a clear appreciation of their employees and permit them to experience a high degree of job satisfaction. A management style that challenges employees and establishes high expectations for their work is essential. Creating a closely knit culture among management and employees is recommended. Employee empowerment will permit decision making to take place closest to the point of action. To keep a union out, employee needs must be identified and met. Management must offer extrinsic and intrinsic rewards to employees. Extrinsic rewards include money, bonuses, and other financial incentives. Intrinsic rewards include recognition, self-esteem, and self-actualizing experiences. The ultimate goal is for employees to be challenged to develop to their fullest potential. These recommendations will assist management to create and maintain a union-free environment.

SOLUTIONS

Multiple Choice:	True/False:	Matching:
1. c	1. False	1. q
2. d	2. False	2. h
3. a	3. True	3. b
4. a	4. True	4. s
5. b	5. False	5. o
6. d	6. True	6. f
7. d	7. False	7. i
8. b	8. False	8. r
9. c	9. True	9. m
10. a	10. True	10. d
11. b	11. False	11. l

12.	d	12.	True	12.	k
13.	a	13.	False	13.	p
14.	b	14.	True	14.	g
15.	c	15.	True	15.	a
16.	d	16.	False	16.	n
17.	c	17.	True	17.	c
18.	a	18.	True	18.	j
19.	d	19.	False	19.	E
20.	b	20.	True	20.	t
21.	a	21.	False		
22.	c	22.	True		
23.	d	23.	True		
24.	d	24.	False		
25.	a	25.	True		
26.	b				
27.	b				
28.	c				
29.	d				
30.	d				

False Statements Made True

1. The primary purpose of the Railway Labor Act is to **avoid service interruptions resulting from disputes between railroads and their operating unions**.

2. Before an injunction may be issued, employers **must** show that lack of an injunction will cause greater harm to the employer than to the union.

5. Most labor-organizing campaigns are undertaken by **employees rather than union organizers**.

7. After the election is held, the winning party will be determined on the basis of the **number of actual votes, not the number of members of the bargaining unit**.

8. The petition to hold representation elections is **usually** initiated by the **union**.

11. Union stewards are normally elected by union members within their department and **serve without union pay**.

13. Most state legislatures **have not** granted public employees the right to strike.

16. Once bargaining begins, an employer **is obligated** to negotiate in good faith with the union's representative over conditions of employment.

19. **An arbitrator** assumes the role of a decision maker and determines what the settlement between the two parties should be.

21. A grievance **should not** be viewed as something to be won or lost from the perspective of the government.

24. Arbitrators are essentially constrained to decide cases based on the wording of the labor agreement, **including** the facts, testimony, and evidence presented at the hearing.

CHAPTER 15

INTERNATIONAL HUMAN RESOURCES MANAGEMENT

A large percentage of the corporations in the United States are engaged in international business. Many of them are multinational corporations (MNCs) and thus have extensive facilities and human resources in foreign countries. The management of MNCs poses special problems. The cultural environment in which MNCs operate is especially important, and managers must be selected carefully and then trained to be effective in a specific environment. Differences among countries in the performance of HRM functions are reviewed briefly as a background for further study.

LEARNING OUTCOMES

After studying this chapter, you should be able to

LEARNING OUTCOME 1	Explain the economic, political, and cultural factors in different countries that HR managers need to consider.
LEARNING OUTCOME 2	Identify the types of organizational forms used for competing internationally.
LEARNING OUTCOME 3	Explain how domestic and international HRM differ.
LEARNING OUTCOME 4	Discuss the staffing process for individuals working internationally.
LEARNING OUTCOME 5	Identify the unique training needs for international assignees and their employees.
LEARNING OUTCOME 6	Identify the characteristics of a good international compensation plan.
LEARNING OUTCOME 7	Reconcile the difficulties of home- and host-country performance appraisals.

| LEARNING OUTCOME 8 | Explain how labor relations differ around the world. |

CHAPTER SUMMARY RELATING TO LEARNING OUTCOMES

LEARNING OUTCOME 1 Economic, political-legal and cultural factors in different parts of the world influence the need for global integration of HR practices as well as the need for local adaptation. These competing forces create a tension for HR managers. The tension is found in how to manage people in a way that is compliant to cultural and political-legal norms while at the same time taking advantage of globally standardized practices.

LEARNING OUTCOME 2 There are four basic ways to organize for global competition: (1) the international corporation is essentially a domestic firm that has leveraged its existing capabilities to penetrate overseas markets; (2) the multinational corporation has fully autonomous units operating in multiple countries in order to address local issues; (3) the global corporation has a worldview but controls all international operations from its home office; and (4) the transnational corporation uses a network structure to balance global and local concerns.

LEARNING OUTCOME 3 International HRM places greater emphasis on a number of responsibilities and functions such as relocation, orientation, and translation services to help employees adapt to a new and different environment outside their own country.

LEARNING OUTCOME Many factors must be considered in the selection and development of employees for international assignments. Hiring host-country nationals or third-country nationals versus sending expatriates is generally less costly. When expatriates are hired, most companies try to minimize their stays. Operations are handed off to host-country nationals as soon as possible.

LEARNING OUTCOME 5 Once an expatriate is selected, an intensive training and development program is essential to qualify that person and his or her spouse and family for the assignment. Wherever possible, development should extend beyond information and orientation training to include sensitivity training and field experiences which will enable the manager to understand cultural differences better. Those in charge of the international programs should provide the help managers need with the career development risks they face, reentry problems, and culture shock. E-mail, instant messaging, and videoconferencing are making it easier for companies to stay in touch with their expatriates

LEARNING OUTCOME 6 Compensation systems should support the overall strategic intent of the organization but be customized for local conditions. Compensation plans must give expatriates an incentive to leave the United States; meet standard of living, health care, and safety needs; provide for the education of their children, if necessary; and facilitate their repatriation.

LEARNING OUTCOME 7   Although home-country managers frequently have formal responsibility for appraising individuals on foreign assignments, they may not be able to fully understand an expatriate's experiences because geographical distances pose communication problems. Host-country managers may be in the best position to observe day-to-day performance but may be biased by cultural factors and may not have a view of the organization as a whole. To balance the pros and cons of home-country and host-country evaluations, performance evaluation that combines the two sources of appraisal information is one option.

LEARNING OUTCOME   In many European countries—Germany, for one—employee representation is established by law. Organizations typically negotiate the agreement with the union at a national level, frequently with government intervention. In other countries, union activity is prohibited or limited to only large companies. European unions have much more political power than many other unions around the world, although their power has declined somewhat due to globalization forces. The International Confederation of Free Trade Unions (IDFTU), European Trade Union Confederation (ETUC), and International Labour Organization (ILO) are among the major worldwide organizations endeavoring to improve the conditions of workers.

REVIEW QUESTIONS

Multiple Choice

Choose the letter of the word or phrase that best completes each statement.

Learning Outcome (LO)

LO 1 _____   1. Communications, religion, values and ideologies, education, and the social structure of a country are examples of
    a. a cultural environnent.
    b. an economic environnent.
    c. employee and customer rights.
    d. a physical environment.

LO 1 _____   2. The country in which an international business operates is the
    a. third-world country.
    b. domestic country.
    c. home country.
    d. host country.

LO 2 _____   3. A multinational firm that maintains control of operations back in the home office can be viewed as a
      a. domestic corporation.
      b. global corporation.
      c. polycentric organization.
      d. geocentric organization.

LO 2 _____   4. The type of organization that attempts to achieve the local responsiveness of a multinational corporation while also achieving the efficiencies of a global firm is a(n)
      a. domestic business.
      b. global business.
      c. transnational corporation.
      d. international organization.

LO 4 _____   5. Natives of a country other than the home country or the host country are
      a. home-country nationals.
      b. expatriates.
      c. third-country nationals.
      d. all of the above.

LO 4 _____   6. The following are different sources of employees with whom to staff international operations, *except*
      a. preferential union shops.
      b. home-country nationals.
      c. host-country nationals.
      d. third-country nationals.

LO 4 _____   7. Natives of the host country who manage international operations are known as
      a. expatriate managers.
      b. third-country nationals.
      c. global managers.
      d. host-country nationals.

LO 4 _____   8. A document issued by a government granting authority to a foreign individual to seek employment in that government's country is a
      a. contract.
      b. work permit or visa.
      c. passport.
      d. green card.

LO 4 _____   9. In the early stages of global expansion, organizations often use _____ to work with local governments.
   a. host-country nationals
   b. third-country nationals
   c. home-country nationals
   d. none of the above

LO 4 _____   10. A major source of trained labor in European nations is
   a. apprenticeship training programs.
   b. translation programs.
   c. job analysis programs.
   d. orientation programs.

LO 4 _____   11. Foreign workers invited to come to a country to perform needed labor are usually referred to as
   a. human resources specialists.
   b. operative employees.
   c. guest workers.
   d. immigrants.

LO 4 _____   12. The assembly of people of multiple nationalities who can work together effectively on projects that span multiple countries is a
   a. trade agreement.
   b. domestic work group.
   c. cartel arrangement.
   d. transnational team.

LO 4 _____   13. In selecting foreign employees, to understand the local market a firm should do all of the following *except*
   a. get to know local schools for a source of employees and to build a network for future employees.
   b. build networks among business and government communities.
   c. understand the employees of competitors.
   d. Since developing nations tend to have schools that are superior to those in the U.S., do not offend school officials by trying to help them change.

LO 4 _____   14. The most prevalent reasons for failure among expatriates working in foreign countries are
   a. technical limitations.
   b. family and lifestyle issues.
   c. economic issues.
   d. religious beliefs.

LO 5 _____ 15. Most executives agree that the biggest problem for the foreign business traveler is
  a. exchange rate conversion.
  b. communicating in different languages.
  c. strategic planning.
  d. accepting bribes.

LO 5 _____ 16. Managerial attitudes and behaviors are influenced by the society in which managers have
  a. job evaluation.
  b. received their education and training.
  c. performance appraisals.
  d. job analysis backgrounds.

LO 5 _____ 17. Studying cultural differences can be helpful to managers in identifying and understanding cultural
  a. augmented skills and the balance-sheet approach.
  b. core skills and guest workers.
  c. work attitudes and motivation.
  d. work permits and work certificates.

LO 5 _____ 18. A disorientation that causes perpetual stress experienced by people who settle overseas for extended periods is
  a. culture shock.
  b. culture environnent.
  c. foreign exchange.
  d. social culture disease.

LO 5 _____ 19. Helping employees make the transition back home is
  a. life-planning.
  b. localization.
  c. debriefing.
  d. repatriation.

LO 5 _____ 20. According to a recent survey, what percentage of expatriates believed that their careers had not advanced after returning home?
  a. 40.
  b. 50.
  c. 60.
  d. 70.

LO 6 _____   21. To be effective, an international compensation program must
  a. provide an incentive to leave the United States.
  b. facilitate reentry home.
  c. be in writing.
  d. do all of the above.

LO 6 _____   22. A compensation system designed to equal the purchasing power in a person's home country is a
  a. job analysis program.
  b. balance-sheet approach to management.
  c. job description.
  d. job specification.

LO 6 _____   23. Under which pay system, expatriates are given a portion of their pay in local currency to cover day-to-day expenses?
  a. split-pay.
  b. balance-sheet approach.
  c. home-based pay.
  d. localization.

LO 6 _____   24. Compensation that is equivalent to that earned by employees in the country where the expatriate is assigned is
  a. a COLA.
  b. incentive pay.
  c. host-based pay.
  d. home-based pay.

LO 7 _____   25. Because expatiate assignments are very costly, many HR Managers are increasingly under pressure to calculate the
  a. return on investment of these assignments.
  b. retention costs of these assignments.
  c. third-country national costs of these assignments.
  d. replacement costs of these assignments.

LO 7 _____   26. Although the home-country and host-country superiors may tell an expatriate how well he or she is doing, it is also important for expatriates to provide feedback regarding
  a. the support they are receiving.
  b. obstacles they face.
  c. suggestions they have about the assignment.
  d. all of the above.

LO 8 _____ 27. Which country only has one union?
     a. China.
     b. India.
     c. Japan.
     d. South Korea.

LO 8 _____ 28. The most active of the international union organizations has been the
     a. International Trade Union Confederation.
     b. All-China Federation of Trade Unions.
     c. International Trade Corporation.
     d. Global Union.

LO 8 _____ 29. Which of the following organizations has had the greatest impact on the rights of workers throughout the world?
     a. International Confederation of Free Trade Unions.
     b. All-China Federation of Trade Unions.
     c. International Trade Corporation.
     d. International Labour Organization.

LO 8 _____ 30. A higher form of worker participation in management is found in Germany where representation of labor on the board of directors of a company is required by law. This arrangement is known as
     a. codetermination.
     b. joint venturing.
     c. legitimate power.
     d. self-managed teams.

True/False

Identify the following statements as True or False.

Learning Outcome (LO)

LO 1 _____ 1. The international corporation is essentially a domestic firm that builds on its existing capabilities to penetrate home markets.

LO 1 _____ 2. To balance a "global/local" dilemma, a transnational corporation uses a network structure that coordinates specialized facilities positioned around the world.

LO 3 _____ 3. International HRM is the same as domestic HRM in all aspects.

LO 3 _____ 4. All large corporations have a part-time staff of human resources specialists devoted to assisting in the globalization process.

LO 4 _____ 5. Third-country nationals are natives of a country other than the home country or the host country.

LO 4 _____ 6. Recently there has been a trend to use only expatriates in the lower management positions.

LO 4 _____ 7. Companies starting operations in developing nations have sometimes partnered with local schools to bring about improvements and provide a source of present and future employees.

LO 4 _____ 8. The employment of non-nationals throughout the globe may involve lower direct labor costs.

LO 4 _____ 9. In the United States, managers tend to emphasize seniority with the most-senior person getting the job.

LO 4 _____ 10. One way to improve the success of expatriate assignments is to provide training for spouses in the process.

LO 4 _____ 11. Core skills are considered critical to an employee's success abroad.

LO 4 _____ 12. The biggest mistake managers can make is to assume that people are different everywhere.

LO 4 _____ 13. Demand for expatriates is growing rapidly.

LO 4 _____ 14. Working abroad tends to increase a person's responsibilities and influence within the organization.

LO 5 _____ 15. When compared with the Japanese, Americans may feel more loyalty to their organizations.

LO 5 _____ 16. One of the important dimensions of leadership is the degree to which managers invite employee participation in decision making.

LO 5 _____ 17. One of the most frequent causes of an employee's failure to complete an international assignment is personal and family stress.

LO 5 _____ 18. Repatriation is the process of helping an employee make the transition back home from an international assignment.

LO 5 _____ 19. All companies have career development programs designed for repatriating employees.

LO 5 _____ 20. More companies are making an effort to keep in touch with expatriates while they are abroad, which has been easier with email, instant messaging, and videoconferencing.

LO 6 _____ 21. One of the most complex areas of international HRM is compensation.

LO 6 _____ 22. Host-country employees are generally paid on the basis of productivity, time spent on the job, or a combination of these factors.

LO 7 _____ 23. HR Managers are increasingly under pressure to calculate the return on investment on expatriate assignments.

LO 8 _____ 24. Because for most companies, labor is their largest cost, it plays a prime role in international HR decision making.

LO 8 _____ 25. The collective bargaining process can vary widely among countries, especially with regard to the role that government plays.

Matching

Match each term with the proper definition.

Terms

a. augmented skills
b. balance-sheet approach
c. codetermination
d. core skills
e. cultural environment
f. culture shock
g. expatriates, home-country nationals
h. failure rate
i. global compensation system
j. global corporation
k. global manager
l. guest workers
m. home-based pay
n. host-based pay

o. host country
p. host-country nationals
q. international corporation
r. localization
s. multinational corporation (MNC)
t. repatriation
u. split pay
v. third-country nationals
w. transnational corporation
x. transnational teams
y. work permit, or visa

Definitions

_____ 1. foreign workers invited into a foreign labor market to perform needed labor.

_____ 2. perceptual stress experienced by people who settle overseas.

_____ 3. firm with independent business units operating in multiple countries.

_____ 4. skills helpful in facilitating the efforts of expatriate managers

_____ 5. natives of the host country.

_____ 6. representation of labor on the board of directors of a company.

_____ 7. firm that has integrated worldwide operations through a centralized home office.

_____ 8. compensation system designed to match the purchasing power of a person's home country.

_____ 9. government document granting a foreign individual the right to seek employment.

_____ 10. country in which an international corporation operates.

_____ 11. employees from the home country who are sent on international assignment.

_____ 12. communication, religion, values and ideologies, education, and social structure of a country.

_____ 13. domestic firm that uses its existing capabilities to move into overseas markets.

_____ 14. teams composed of members of multiple nationalities working on projects that span multiple countries.

_____ 15. skills considered critical in an employee's success abroad.

_____ 16. firm that attempts to balance local responsiveness and global scale via a network of specialized operating units.

_____ 17. manager equipped to run an international business.

_____ 18. percentage of expatriates who do not perform satisfactorily.

_____ 19. natives of a country other than the home country or the host country.

_____ 20. process that helps employees make the transition back home after a foreign assignment.

_____ 21. expatriate pay comparable to that earned by employees in a host country.

_____ 22. pay based on an expatriate's home country's compensation practices.

_____ 23. adapting pay and other compensation benefits to match that of a particular country.

_____ 24. A centralized pay system whereby host-county employees are offered a full range of training programs, benefits, and pay comparable with a firm's domestic employee but adjusted for local differences.

_____ 25. A system whereby expatriates are given a portion of their pay in the local currency to cover their day-to-day expenses and a portion of their pay in their home currency to safeguard their earnings from changes in inflation or foreign exchange rates.

Internet Exercises

How can you bridge the gap to minimize culture shock?
http://www.findarticles.com/p/articles/mi_m0DTI/is_7_31/ai_104079169.
What are the challenges of international human resources management?
http://www.findarticles.com/p/articles/mi_m3495/is_n3_v42/ai_19445784.

How to Prepare for an International Assignment for a Multinational Corporation

In the recruiting and selection process for an international assignment, you should understand the preparation required for this opportunity. This would include an understanding of the host nation's culture, political and legal framework, and customs. Once selected, you should undertake an intensive training and development program. Development should extend beyond information and orientation training to include sensitivity training and field experiences that will enable you to better understand cultural differences. Seek the support of the person(s) in charge of the international program in order to avoid career development risks, reentry problems, and culture shock.

The socialization process involving the culture and customs is an important orientation objective. To understand fully the challenges of the international assignment, you should be able to adapt to the methodology of the foreign country's business practices. Finally, do not impose American values and business practices in the foreign country. Preparation includes understanding the business customs and practices that exist in the foreign culture.

SOLUTIONS

Multiple Choice:	True/False:	Matching:
1. a	1. False	1. l
2. d	2. True	2. f
3. b	3. False	3. s
4. c	4. False	4. a
5. c	5. True	5. p
6. a	6. False	6. c
7. d	7. False	7. j
8. b	8. True	8. b
9. c	9. False	9. y
10. a	10. True	10. o
11. c	11. True	11. g
12. d	12. False	12. e
13. d	13. True	13. q
14. b	14. True	14. x
15. b	15. False	15. d
16. b	16. True	16. w
17. c	17. True	17. k
18. a	18. True	18. h
19. d	19. False	19. v
20. c	20. True	20. t
21. d	21. True	21. n
22. b	22. True	22. m
23. a	23. True	23. r
24. c	24. True	24. i
25. a	25. True	25. u
26 d		
27. a		
28. a		
29. d		
30. a		

False Statements Made True

1. The international corporation is essentially a domestic firm that builds on its existing capabilities to penetrate **overseas** markets.

3. International HRM **differs from** domestic HRM in **many ways**.

4. **Most** large corporations have a **full-time** staff of human resources **managers** devoted to assisting in the globalization process.

6. Recently there has been a trend to use only expatriates in the **top** management positions.

9. In the United States, managers tend to emphasize **merit**, with the **best-qualified** person getting the job.

12. The biggest mistake managers can make is to assume that people are **the same** everywhere.

15. When compared with the Japanese, Americans may feel **little** loyalty to their organizations.

19. **Unfortunately, not all** companies have career development programs designed for repatriating employees.

CHAPTER 16

CREATING HIGH-PERFORMANCE
WORK SYSTEMS

High-performance work systems are integral for HR practices that maximize employee knowledge, skill, commitment, and flexibility. The system begins with implementing empowered work teams to perform key business processes. Training of team members is paramount, and reward systems are used to motivate behavior. When the subsystems complement one another, the result is both an internal and external fit that produces a holistic system. For the system to function effectively, it must have top management as well as labor union support. The result is a high-performance work system that benefits both the employees and the organization.

LEARNING OUTCOMES

After studying this chapter, you should be able to

LEARNING OUTCOME 1	Discuss the underlying principles of high-performance work systems.
LEARNING OUTCOME 2	Identify the components that make up a high-performance work system.
LEARNING OUTCOME 3	Describe how the components fit together and support strategy.
LEARNING OUTCOME 4	Recommend processes for implementing high-performance work systems.
LEARNING OUTCOME 5	Discuss the outcomes for both employees and the organization.

CHAPTER SUMMARY RELATING TO LEARNING OUTCOMES

LEARNING OUTCOME 1　　High-performance work systems are specific combinations of HR practices, work structures, and processes that maximize the knowledge, skills, commitment, and flexibility of employees. The systems are TQM oriented and based on the principles of shared information, knowledge development, performance-reward linkages, and egalitarianism and employee engagement.

LEARNING OUTCOME 2　　High-performance work systems are composed of several interrelated components. Team members are carefully selected and undergo extensive training, including cross training, and often share leadership duties. Typically, the system begins with designing empowered work teams to carry out key business processes. Integrated information technology systems can help ensure that employees have the information they need to make timely and productive decisions. To align the interests of employees with those of the organization, the reward systems associated with high-performance work systems are performance based, and often include group and organizational incentive pay and sometimes skill-based pay.

LEARNING OUTCOME 3　　The pieces of the system are important only in terms of how they help the entire system function. When all the pieces support and complement one another, high-performance work systems achieve internal fit. When the system is aligned with the competitive priorities of the organization as a whole, it achieves external fit as well.

LEARNING OUTCOME 4　　Implementing high-performance work systems within existing organizations often has to be done in stages. The implementation is much more likely to go smoothly if a business case is first made for the HPWS and fully communicated to employees. The support of the firm's top and middle managers is critical, and so too is the support of union representatives and the company's other key groups and divisions. Because firms today gain a competitive advantage primarily from the capabilities of the talent, a company's HR department can be an invaluable partner when it comes to implementing a HPWS. HR personnel can also help establish a transition structure to shepherd the implementation through its various stages and reassure employees they will be successful working in the new system. Once the system is in place, it should be evaluated in terms of its processes, outcomes, sustainability, and ongoing fit with strategic objectives of the organization.

LEARNING OUTCOME 5　　Progressive organizations of all sizes have successfully implemented high-performance work systems. When implemented effectively, high-performance work systems benefit both employees and their organizations. Employees become more engaged and empowered to make decisions, experience greater career growth and satisfaction, and become more valuable contributors to their firms. Organizations benefit from higher productivity, quality, flexibility, and customer satisfaction. These features together can provide a company with a sustainable competitive advantage.

REVIEW QUESTIONS

Multiple Choice

Choose the letter of the word or phrase that best completes each statement.

Learning Outcome (LO)

LO 1 _____   1. The specific combination of human resources practices, work structures, and processes that maximize employee knowledge, skill, commitment, and flexibility is known as
    a. high-performance work systems.
    b. labor-intensive organizations.
    c. self-managed teams.
    d. external integration.

LO 1 _____   2. One of the primary principles that support high-performance work systems is
    a. job turnover linkage.
    b. complacency evolution.
    c. sharing information.
    d. employment transfer linkage.

LO 1 _____   3. The principle that includes selecting the best and the brightest candidates available in the labor market and providing all employees opportunities to continuously hone their talents is
    a. shared information.
    b. egalitarianism.
    c. knowledge development.
    d. external fit.

LO 1 _____   4. Involving employees in decision making and giving them the power to act tends to increase what HR professionals refer to as
    a. shared information.
    b. employee engagement
    c. knowledge development.
    d. external fit.

LO 1 _____   5. When employees pursue outcomes that are mutually beneficial to themselves and the organization, this process is known as the
    a. job-knowledge linkage.
    b. performance-reward linkage.
    c. principle of egalitarianism.
    d. concept of shared information.

LO 1 _____ 6. The concept that eliminates status and power differences and, in the process, increases collaboration and teamwork is
   a. shared information.
   b. performance-reward linkage.
   c. knowledge development.
   d. egalitarianism.

LO 1 _____ 7. Moving power downward in organizations by empowering employees frequently requires
   a. structural changes.
   b. bureaucratic changes.
   c. centralized instruction.
   d. cross-training.

LO 2 _____ 8. Emphasis on teamwork, involvement, and continuous improvement requires that employees develop a broader understanding of work processes performed by others around them rather than rely on just knowing their own jobs through
   a. corporate downsizing.
   b. internal fit.
   c. cross-training.
   d. external fit.

LO 2 _____ 9. High-performance work systems frequently begin with the way
   a. work is designed.
   b. people are hired.
   c. employees are paid.
   d. employees are trained.

LO 2 _____ 10. In order to link pay and performance, high-performance work systems often include some type of
   a. glass ceiling.
   b. employee incentives.
   c. process audit.
   d. external fit.

LO 2 _____ 11. By paying employees on the basis of the number of different job skills they have, high-performance work systems may also incorporate
   a. piece-rate plans.
   b. standard-hour plans.
   c. performance evaluation.
   d. skill-based pay plans.

LO 2 _____ 12. In addition to linking pay and performance, high-performance work systems are based on the principle of
  a. egalitarianism.
  b. process auditing.
  c. cross-functional training.
  d. internal fit.

LO 2 _____ 13. Managers and supervisors in high-performance work systems have the following roles, *except*
  a. coaches.
  b. facilitators.
  c. authoritarian leaders.
  d. integrators of team efforts.

LO 2 _____ 14. An addition to the framework of high-performance work systems, vital to business performance is
  a. centralized management organizations.
  b. rigid organization structures.
  c. authoritarian leadership.
  d. communication and information technologies.

LO 2 _____ 15. High-performance work systems cannot succeed without accurate and timely information, which includes the following, *except*
  a. business plans and goals.
  b. deprivation of core competencies.
  c. unit and corporate operating results.
  d. incipient problems and opportunities.

LO 3 _____ 16. The condition that exists when all internal elements of the work system complement and reinforce each other is
  a. job enlargement.
  b. external fit.
  c. job analysis.
  d. internal fit.

LO 3 _____ 17. A strategy that begins with an analysis and discussion of competitive challenges, organizational value, and the concerns of employees and results in a statement of the strategies being pursued by the organization is known as a(n)
  a. external fit.
  b. process audit.
  c. internal fit.
  d. job evaluation.

LO 4 _____ 18. A model that helps managers assess the strategic alignment of their work systems is the
    a. HR Scorecard.
    b. Theory X Model.
    c. Theory Y Model.
    d. Maslow Model.

LO 4 _____ 19. To get initial commitment to high-performance work systems, managers have to build a case that the changes are needed for the
    a. internal fit.
    b. external fit.
    c. success of the organization.
    d. efficiency of the closed system.

LO 4 _____ 20. Autocratic styles of management and confrontational approaches to labor negotiations are being challenged by more enlightened approaches that promote
    a. adventurous and technological programs.
    b. coercion and communication.
    c. cooperation and collaboration.
    d. conflict and coordination.

LO 4 _____ 21. In order to establish an alliance, managers and labor representatives should try to create a(n)
    a. adversarial system.
    b. "win-win" situation.
    c. balance-sheet approach.
    d. "win-lose" approach.

LO 4 _____ 22. Most labor-management alliances are made legitimate through some tangible symbol of a(n)
    a. informal commitment.
    b. culture icon.
    c. trade agreement.
    d. formal commitment.

LO 4 _____ 23. _____ keeps the parties focused and ensures that democracy and fairness prevail.
    a. coercion
    b. reward systems
    c. evaluation
    d. all of the above

LO 4 _____   24. _____ can have a huge impact impact on how well high-performance work systems are implemented.
a. recruiting
b. allocating too few resources to the effort
c. cooperation and trust
d. recognition and respect

LO 4 _____   25. In which of the following types of firms is building a transition structure least cumbersome?
a. start-up firms
b. growth firms
c. mature firms
d. declining firms

LO 4 _____   26. The evaluation process that focuses on whether the high-performance work system has been implemented as designed is
a. internal fit.
b. performance appraisal.
c. process audit.
d. external fit.

LO 4 _____   27. The advantage of high-performance work systems is that they are
a. flexible and adaptable.
b. autocratic and coercive.
c. divisive in conflict.
d. manipulative and confrontational.

LO 5 _____   28. The following are organizational outcomes that result from using high-performance work systems, *except*
a. lower productivity.
b. lower costs.
c. better responsiveness to customers.
d. higher profitability.

LO 5 _____   29. High-performance work system outcomes can be categorized in terms of either employee concerns or
a. quality-of-work-life issues.
b. job security.
c. competitive challenges.
d. return on investment.

Managing Human Resources

LO 5 _____ 30. Organizations can create a sustainable competitive advantage through people if they focus on four criteria. One of the criteria is
    a. difficult to organize.
    b. cheap.
    c. easy to find.
    d. difficult to imitate.

True/False

Identify the following statements as True or False.

Learning Outcome (LO)

LO 1 _____ 1. Without timely and accurate information about the business, employees can do little more than simply carry out orders and perform their roles in a relatively perfunctory way.

LO 1 _____ 2. When employees are given timely information about business performance, plans, and strategies, they are more likely to make good suggestions for improving the business and to cooperate in major organizational changes.

LO 1 _____ 3. Employees in high-performance work systems need to learn in "real time," on the job, using traditional approaches to solve novel problems.

LO 1 _____ 4. A time-tested adage of management is that the interests of employees and organizations naturally diverge.

LO 1 _____ 5. Productivity can improve when introducing egalitarianism by having people who once worked in opposition begin to work together.

LO 2 _____ 6. High-performance work systems combine various work structures, human resources practices, and management processes to maximize employee performance and well-being.

LO 2 _____ 7. Total quality management and reengineering have driven many organizations to redesign their workflow by focusing on the key business processes that drive voluntary layoffs.

LO 2 _____ 8. Work redesign, in and of itself, does not constitute a high-performance work system.

LO 2 _____ 9. Recruitment tends to be both broad and intensive in order to create the best pool of job candidates.

LO 2 _____ 10. Training is focused on ensuring that employees have the skills needed to assume greater responsibility in a high-performance work environment.

LO 2 _____ 11. Because high-performance work systems ask many different things from employees, it is easy to isolate one single compensation approach that works for everyone.

LO 2 _____ 12. The open-pay plan is yet another way to create a more egalitarian environment that discourages employee involvement and commitment.

LO 2 _____ 13. In a growing number of organizations, leadership is shared among team members.

LO 2 _____ 14. The richest form of communication occurs face-to-face between sender and receiver.

LO 2 _____ 15. High-performance work systems can succeed without timely and accurate communications.

LO 3 _____ 16. External fit occurs when all the internal elements of the work system complement and reinforce one another.

LO 3 _____ 17. A situation in which the high-performance work system supports the organization's goals and strategies is known as internal fit.

LO 4 _____ 18. One of the best ways to communicate the business's needs is to show employees the business's current performance and capabilities.

LO 4 _____ 19. Two-way communication can result in better decisions and it may help to diminish the fears and concerns of employees.

LO 4 _____ 20. Building commitment to high-performance work systems is a one-time activity.

LO 4 _____ 21. The bottom-up approach communicates manager support and clarity, while the top-down approach ensures employee acceptance and commitment.

LO 5 _____ 22. A potential benefit to employees from high-performance work systems is they are likely to be more satisfied and find that their needs for growth are more fully met.

LO 5 _____ 23. Implementing high-performance work systems is an easy task, even though systems are complex, and they require a good deal of close partnering among executives, line managers, HR professionals, union representatives, and employees.

LO 5 _____ 24. Because high-performance work systems are simple to implement, organizations that are successful are simple to copy.

LO 5 _____ 25. The four criteria for a sustainable advantage covered in chapter two also apply to organizations with high-performance systems.

Matching

Match each term with the proper definition.

Terms

a. external fit
b. high-performance work system (HPWS)

c. internal fit
d. process audit

Definitions

_____ 1. situation in which all the internal elements of the work system complement and reinforce one another.

_____ 2. situation in which the work system supports the organization's goals and strategies.

_____ 3. specific combination of HR practices, work structures, and processes that maximizes employee knowledge, skill, commitment, and flexibility.

_____ 4. determining whether the high-performance work system has been implemented as designed.

Internet Exercises

How to manage machine downtime to be more cost effective.
http://www.findarticles.com/p/articles/mi_qa3713/is_200404/ai_n9398989.

What is the result of a high-performance work system in the insurance industry?
http://www.findarticles.com/p/articles/mi_qa3615/is_200504/ai_n13616468.

How to Apply High-Performance Work Systems to Small-, Medium-, and Large-Scale Organizations

High-performance work systems (HPWSs) have become a recent trend for organizations in order to become more efficient and profitable. HPWSs can be defined as a specific combination of human resources practices, work structures, and processes that maximize employee knowledge, skill, commitment, and flexibility. The principles of HPWS apply in small and medium-sized organizational work settings as well as in large organizations. For example, progressive organizations of all sizes have successfully implemented team-based work systems, adopted staffing practices that select high-quality employees, developed training programs that continually update employee skills, and utilized compensation practices that support specific organizational goals. The important element is that these organizations have accomplished these tasks in a coordinated and integrative manner. In smaller organizations, a system approach to organizational design is adopted to combine human resources practices, work structures, and processes that effectively utilize employee competencies. In these small businesses, the human resources function is the responsibility of line management. The line manager must recruit and select among a pool of talent, orient and train these individuals, and assume many of the human resources functions. As the organization grows, the staff function of human resources management becomes a reality for the human resources department that accepts the responsibilities that have been developed in this course.

Regardless of the organization's size, evidence suggests that the use of high-performance work systems has led to increased profitability. Research has shown that human resources practices are aggressive activities that create a stronger competitive advantage relative to other firms. Today, the human resources plan is an integrative approach in developing a holistic system with other departments of small, medium-sized, and large organizations. An objective is to recruit and select the most qualified individuals to perform the necessary tasks to achieve organizational goals.

SOLUTIONS

Multiple Choice:	True/False:	Matching:
1. a	1. True	1. c
2. c	2. True	2. a
3. c	3. False	3. b
4. b	4. True	4. d
5. b	5. True	
6. d	6. True	
7. a	7. False	
8. c	8. True	
9. a	9. True	
10. b	10. True	
11. d	11. False	
12. a	12. False	

223

13.	c	13.	True
14.	d	14.	True
15.	b	15.	False
16.	d	16.	False
17.	a	17.	False
18.	a	18.	True
19.	c	19.	True
20.	c	20.	False
21.	b	21.	False
22.	d	22.	True
23.	d	23.	False
24.	b	24.	False
25.	a	25.	True
26.	c		
27.	a		
28.	a		
29.	c		
30.	d		

False Statements Made True

3. Employees in high-performance work systems need to learn in "real time" on the job, using **innovative new** approaches to solve novel problems.

7. Total quality management and reengineering have driven many organizations to redesign their workflow by focusing on the key business processes that drive **customer value**.

11. Because high-performance work systems ask many different things from employees, it is **difficult** to isolate one single compensation approach that works for everyone.

12. The open-pay plan is yet another way to create a more egalitarian environment that **encourages** employee involvement and commitment.

15. High-performance work systems **cannot** succeed without timely and accurate communications.

16. **Internal** fit occurs when all the internal elements of the work system complement and reinforce one another.

17. A situation in which the high-performance work system supports the organization's goals and strategies is known as **external** fit.

20. Building commitment to high-performance work systems is **an ongoing** activity.

21. The **top-down** approach communicates manager support and clarity, while the **bottom-up** approach ensures employee acceptance and commitment.

23. Implementing high-performance work systems is **a difficult** task **because** systems are complex, and they require a good deal of close partnering among executives, line managers, HR professionals, union representatives, and employees.

24. Because high-performance work systems are **difficult** to implement, organizations that are successful are **difficult** to copy.